The In ...ns of
New England

BIBLIOGRAPHICAL SERIES
*The Newberry Library Center
for the History of the American Indian*

General Editor
Francis Jennings

Assistant Editor
William R. Swagerty

The Center Is Supported by Grants from

The National Endowment for the Humanities
The Ford Foundation
The W. Clement and Jessie V. Stone Foundation
The Woods Charitable Fund, Inc.
Mr. Gaylord Donnelley
The Andrew W. Mellon Foundation
The Robert R. McCormick Charitable Trust
The John D. and Catherine T. McArthur Foundation

The Indians of New England

A Critical Bibliography

NEAL SALISBURY

Published for the Newberry Library

Indiana University Press

BLOOMINGTON

Manufactured in the United States of America

Library of Congress Cataloging in Publication Data

Salisbury, Neal.
    The Indians of New England.

    (Bibliographical series / The Newberry Library Center for the History of the American Indian)
    Includes index.
    1. Indians of North America — New England — Bibliography. I. Title. II. Series: Bibliographical series (Newberry Library. Center for the History of the American Indian)
Z1209.2.U52N377 [E78.N5] 016.974′00497 81–48085
ISBN 0–253–32981–7 (pbk.)   AACR2
1 2 3 4 5 86 85 84 83 82

CONTENTS

ACKNOWLEDGMENTS

Though the persons who generously furnished suggestions, advance manuscripts, and offprints are too many to list individually, I would like to single out Professor Willard Walker for sharing his unpublished bibliography on Maine-Maritime Indians with me; the staffs of the Newberry Library and the William Allan Neilson Library, Smith College, particularly the latter's Inter-Library Loan Service, for assistance in procuring many of the titles listed (and not listed) here; and James Axtell for contributing some fine scholarly and literary touches to the final manuscript.

PREFACE

In 1524, Giovanni da Verrazzano sailed into Narragansett Bay during his exploration of the eastern North American coast for the King of France. He was so favorably impressed by the land and, particularly, the native inhabitants ("These people are the most beautiful and have the most civil customs that we have found on this voyage"), that he remained for fifteen days and named the place "Refugio." Thus was recorded the first known observation of Indians in New England, and the beginning of an ever-expanding body of writing about them. It should be added that this literature has not always depicted them so positively. Verrazzano himself described the Abenaki he later encountered in starkly opposite terms, and negative images of ignoble "savages" have subsequently appeared more frequently than their "noble" counterparts. Even more striking than the content and the stereotypical quality of these images, is the fact that, regardless of when they have appeared, they have referred primarily to the colonial period—that is to those Indians who were conquered in order to make room for the establishment of European societies on their soil. This means that since the colonial period, there has been a growing discrepancy between the Indians actually inhabiting New England at a given time and those appearing in the scholarly literature. This discrepancy reflects both the decreasing power and visibility of native peoples after the colonial period and the peculiar ways in which historians and other writers have perceived the region's past.

A few of the earliest Puritan writers who interacted frequently with semi-autonomous Indians left relatively useful, though heavily biased, cultural descriptions, as William S. Simmons has recently demonstrated [202]. (Simmons's generalization is even more appropriate for those writers who preceded or opposed the Puritans.) As colonial expansion led to intensified Indian-English conflict in the southern New England colonies, Puritan authors tended increasingly to interpret and justify their missionary, diplomatic, and military actions and, decreasingly, to provide insights into the culture, motives, and other perspectives of the natives. Thus most of the writing produced in southern New England from the time of the Pequot War (1637) to the end of the seventeenth century contributed to a massive rationale and myth of conquest in which the land-hungry colonists' victory over native efforts to resist was depicted as one of Divine Providence over the "savage" forces of Satan. In the following century, the principal contributors were missionaries who described their efforts to complete the cultural and mental side of the conquest process. Their despair over the continued manifestations of "savagery" among their charges reflected the reality of the latter's continued cultural autonomy in the face of material deprivation and segregation from the mainstream of New England society.

To the north, in what is now Vermont, New Hampshire, and Maine, the process of conquest, and hence the literature describing it, followed a somewhat different course. To begin with, the north remained a frontier area throughout the colonial period and so attracted far fewer pens than did the relatively cosmopolitan southern colonies. It was also a region caught in the imperial crossfire between Britain and France. But the French presence was always minimal and, therefore, benign in its effects on the natives whereas the English sought, as in the south, to seize Indian lands in order to establish settlements. Thus French writings reflected Simmons's generalizations about some of the earliest Puritan writers while English contributions represent the extension of the conquest myth into this region.

The passing of the colonial period did not bring an abatement of interest in its Indians. On the contrary, the onset of the Industrial Revolution, immigration from Ireland, and emigration to the West only heightened Yankee nostalgia for the romanticism of New England's own frontier era. As a result, histories of the English conquest proliferated on an unprecedented scale. Whether the Indians were portrayed as brutal "savages" or more thoroughly and sympathetically, the result was always a cosmic struggle between "civilization and "barbarism" in which the latter's demise was inevitable. Apart from this abundance of melodrama, the nostalgia of the nineteenth century had some positive effects for subsequent generations of scholars. Besides a handful of valuable histories, it brought concerted efforts throughout the region to preserve and systematize the colonial record. State and local histories were published, some of which remain valuable for their insights into Indian-White relations at the local level and for including documents that have since been lost. A vast number of documents were edited and published either by themselves or in the serial collections of the several state historical societies and many more were preserved and remain available in the libraries of these societies and in state archives. As a result of all these efforts, the documentary record of Indian history in the colonial period is one of considerable scope and magnitude.

Students of nineteenth-century Indian history, on the other hand, are not so fortunate. As New England's Yankees recorded and dramatized the colonial past, the region's living Indians virtually disappeared from literary and official view. During and following the Revolution, many had emigrated in hopes of retaining a measure of communal autonomy. Those who remained in the region were noticed only occasionally when deplorable conditions led a native leader like William Apess or a conscientious official like John Milton Earle to publicize their plight.

The beginning of the twentieth century brought a transformation in the writing of history as amateur and professional authors gave way to academic historians. For the first two-thirds of the century, Indians were virtually absent in historical writing about New England. Even for the colonial period, they were noted only in passing by "imperial school" historians like Charles M. Andrews and not at all by explicators of "the Puritan mind" like Perry Miller. On the other hand, a renewed if minimal awareness of an Indian *presence* began to be acknowledged. This awareness was initially prompted by the larger concern among anthropologists and others that native cultures throughout the United States had to be recorded before they disappeared forever. Though most assumed that such a disappearance had already occurred in the east, one—Frank G. Speck—did not. Speck spent the first half of the century recording a wealth of detail on surviving native traditions in New England and elsewhere in eastern North America.

Even as Speck wrote, a revitalization of native communities and cultures in New England was underway as part of a larger national trend. This trend accelerated after World War II and especially with the political upheavals of the 1960s. Whether responding favorably or unfavorably, non-Indians have tended to view the recent activism, particularly the pressing of land claims cases, as a new form of Indian "warfare." The result has been a large amount of media attention and, therefore, an awareness of their Indian contemporaries by the general public for the first time since the colonial period. Though most of the recent writing is journalism that has quickly become dated, the handful of more lasting contributions included in this bibliography signal an important development in the history of the literature. And while public awareness of today's Indians has been growing, scholars have rediscovered the native peoples of the past. They, too, have been affected by contemporary politics as well as by developments within the academy, particularly the rise of an interdisciplinary "ethnohistory" among both historians and anthropologists. But while great strides have been made in presenting the natives on their own terms, rather than those of the dominant culture, ethnohistorians have fixed their attention exclusively on the colonial period, reminding us with some irony of that earlier Yankee nostalgia.

Though the chronological and topical distribution of works cited in this bibliography necessarily reflects the proclivities of their authors, the essay has been constructed so as to provide a framework for viewing the history of Indians in New England as a whole. Thus the colonial period is presented as merely one of several, and most of the titles appear in connection with one of the periods and none under non-historical categories. Hopefully, this will encourage readers to think of New England Indian history as a continuum rather than in terms of one or another of its more familiar aspects. If we can begin to think this way, future bibliographies on the subject may well exhibit greater balance.

A few words are also in order regarding the territorial scope of this bibliography. "New England" is a Euro-American designation that bears no inherent relationship to the political and cultural boundaries that have existed at one time or another among native peoples who happen to fall within it. The term was first applied by John Smith in 1614 to the coastline between Monhegan Island and Cape Cod and expanded thereafter until it encompassed what are now the six states of the far northeastern United States. This essay will focus on literature pertaining to Indians within the region as most recently defined, but with some flexibility to accord with the boundaries dividing Indians themselves. Thus the Indians of eastern Long Island, who have traditionally been most closely related to those of the Connecticut coast, are included here.

An additional adjustment has been made because Indians have crossed the elusive New England boundary on many occasions and in both directions. Works on Indians who left the region during and soon after the colonial period for Quebec, New York, and Wisconsin are included in this essay insofar as they follow the emigrés to their new homes. Indian immigrants, such as the Mahicans in the eighteenth century and the Micmacs in the twentieth, are discussed only from the time of their arrivals.

The most obvious discrepancy between the entity, "New England," and the ethnographic realities of its Indian peoples is the traditionally sharp dividing line between north and south. The split originated about 600 years before European contact when the spread of agriculture divided the region's inhabitants along demographic, social, and, to a significant extent, cultural lines. Then, during the colonial period, the populous, agricultural south attracted most of the land-hungry settlers who came from England while the hunting peoples of the north retained important ties to France. Still later, Indians in the south were directly affected by urbanization and the rise of commercial and industrial capitalism while those in the north remained relatively isolated from the more visible manifestations of social and economic change. However, this dichotomous quality in the New England Indians' history has been counterbalanced by the linguistic, cultural, and political ties that predated the arrival of Europeans, and by their common experience as European and, particularly, United States subjects.

RECOMMENDED WORKS

For the Beginner

[24]   T.J.C. Brasser, "The Coastal Algonkians."

[95]   Jo Jo Hunt et al., *Report on Terminated and Non-federally Recognized Indians,* Section II B.

[101] Francis Jennings, *The Invasion of America.*

[236] Bruce G. Trigger, ed., *Northeast.*

[241] Willard Walker, et al., "A Chronological Account of the Wabanaki Confederacy."

For a Basic Library

[8]   James Axtell, *The European and the Indian.*

[15]   Harold Blodgett, *Samson Occom.*

[89]   Jeanne Guillemin, *Urban Renegades.*

[92]   George L. Hicks and David I. Kertzer, "Making a Middle Way."

[95]   Jo Jo Hunt, et al., *Report on Terminated and Nonfederally Recognized Indians.*

BIBLIOGRAPHICAL ESSAY

Tribal and Regional Histories

Presumably because "New England" as a distinct entity has never been a reality for Indians, no one has attempted a single volume history of native peoples in the region. Students seeking the kind of overview that such a history would provide should begin with the tribal essays in the *Northeast* volume of the *Handbook of North American Indians* [236] by Erikson [76], Snow [208], Day [62], Simmons [199], and Brasser [26], plus the essays by Salwen and Conkey, et al. [190] [46], which together cover the Indians of southern New England. All the essays include discussions of language, territory, culture at the beginning of European contact, synonymy, and sources, with most attention to history and culture. The essays are valuable for the basic data they provide, particularly on demography and political groupings, subjects of much misunderstanding in earlier works by historians and anthropologists alike.

Besides the *Handbook* essays, a few studies present comprehensive histories of specific groups or regions from the colonial period to the recent past. T. J. C. Brasser, "The Coastal Algonkians" [24] provides a concise summary, including political and military events as well as cultural change. Brasser's periodization of the colonial period into "traders," "settlers," and "integrative" phases is especially effective. But his essay is misleadingly titled in that it concerns coastal Algonquians from southern New England southward and has little appli-

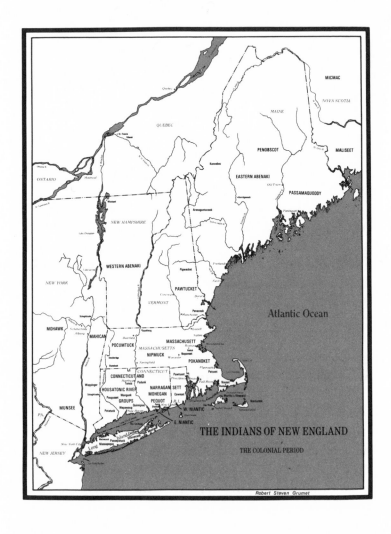

MICMAC

NOVA SCOTIA

MAINE

QUEBEC

PENOBSCOT

MALISEET

EASTERN ABENAKI

PASSAMAQUODDY

ONTARIO

NEW HAMPSHIRE

WESTERN ABENAKI

Pigwacket

PAWTUCKET

NEW YORK

VERMONT

Atlantic Ocean

MOHAWK

MAHICAN

MASSACHUSETT

POCUMTUCK

MASSACHUSETTS

NIPMUCK

POKANOKET

CONNECTICUT AND

HOUSATONIC RIVER

NARRAGANSETT

GROUPS

MOHEGAN

MUNSEE

PEQUOT

W. NIANTIC

PA.

E. NIANTIC

THE INDIANS OF NEW ENGLAND

NEW JERSEY

THE COLONIAL PERIOD

Robert Steven Grumet

cation to the very different experiences of the Abenaki peoples to the north. The remaining histories in this group are more narrowly focused but with greater depth. Ethel Boissevain's *The Narragansett People* [18] is a readable introduction to that group's history. For the little known eighteenth and nineteenth centuries, it should be supplemented by Campbell and LaFantasie's critical account, "Scattered to the Winds of Heaven" [31]. Francis G. Hutchins, *Mashpee* [96], presents a good summary of that community's fascinating history, drawing on source materials never before used by scholars. The account becomes confused and even contradictory at the very end, however, when the author tries to reconcile it with a defense of the recent court decision denying the Mashpee people federal recognition as a tribe. Brasser has written a history of the *Indians of Long Island* [23] which is especially valuable for demonstrating both the links and the differences between the native peoples of the island and those of the adjacent mainland. An outstanding older history is John W. De Forest, *History of the Indians of Connecticut* [63], a meticulously detailed narrative of Indians in that state through the mid-nineteenth century. It is now outdated in its demography and its ethnography and, like most works of its time, views Indian-White relations as a tragic conflict between barbarism and civility. But De Forest does denounce many English injustices and the thoroughness and relative balance of his presentation allow modern readers to form their own conclusions.

Before Europeans

A recent development in the archaeology of northeastern North America has been the recognition that the cultures encountered by the first Europeans during the sixteenth century were the results of centuries, if not millennia, of successful *in situ* adaptations rather than of recent migrations, as had formerly been assumed. This recognition of continuity between precontact and early colonial cultures is reflected in some of the recent archaeological literature pertaining to New England.

The starting point for anyone approaching the archaeology of a region is the surveys of current literature. In such surveys the most recent discoveries are incorporated into the larger picture as it is currently understood by specialists. For the northeast, the best survey as of now is not a single article but rather the sequence of articles in Trigger [236] by Funk [83], Tuck [238], and Fitting [79], plus Dean Snow's "Late Prehistory of the East Coast" [209]. Together these four essays provide an ideal introduction to the history of New England before the arrival of Europeans, plus the vital background needed for understanding the peoples and cultures of the early colonial period. The first three summarize developments for their respective periods, generally taking middle-of-the-road positions between traditional and innovative paradigms. Fitting says little about New England specifically but this can be attributed at least in part to the paucity of evidence for the period he covers. What makes the sequence especially useful for students of Indian history is Snow's presentation of coastal Algonquian territoriality as defined by river drainage systems. The fact that political boundaries were marked by the watersheds between river systems, rather than by the rivers themselves, is not only consistent with what is known archaeologically about pre-contact subsistence and settlement patterns but constitutes an important corrective to much that has been written about Indian politics during the early colonial period.

One survey of a single locale that carries into the early colonial period is Dena Dincauze's "An Introduction to Archaeology in the Greater Boston Area" [64]. Dincauze notes how the European invasion is registered in burial and other sites, and suggests ways in which archaeology can enrich our understanding of the badly documented history of native peoples around Massachusetts Bay during the seventeenth century. A far more detailed local survey, William A. Ritchie, *The Archaeology of Martha's Vineyard* [174], draws on the evidence of successive ecological adaptations on that island to construct "a framework for the prehistory of southern New England."

Dean Snow's recently completed *Archaeology of New England* [210] promises to stand for some time as the definitive work on pre-contact New England. This work synthesizes the archaeological evidence on New England and offers a new periodization between the end of the Archaic and the beginning of the colonial era. In his chapter on "The Historic Baseline," Snow not only correlates geographic and political boundaries, as in the essay noted above, but shows how languages and dialects followed the same lines. His study supplants Charles C. Willoughby's long-outmoded *Antiquities of the New England Indians* [252].

The best survey of the New England Algonquian languages and their dialects is in Goddard, "Eastern Algonquian Languages" [85]. Goddard's "Central Algonquian Languages" [84] concludes with a brief discussion that places the languages in the context of the Algonquian family as a whole. Gordon M. Day surveys the major linguistic sources in "Historical Notes on New England Languages" [58]. James Constantine Pilling, *Bibliography of the Algonquian Languages* [167], is an exhaustive survey of these sources and of all pre-1900 publications in, or pertaining to, Algonquian. But his commentaries favor Protestant missionaries so that as insignificant a figure as Abraham Pierson receives more extensive treatment than do such major contributors as Roger Williams and Sébastien Râle. The contribution of Indians to the bridging of the language gap are also underplayed when mentioned at all.

Snow also provides new population estimates for each group on the eve of the colonial period, reasoning from archaeological as well as documentary evidence. His figures, like those offered in other recent works, supplant the earlier, lower estimates in Sherburne F. Cook, *The Indian Population of New England in the Seventeenth Century* [50], which overlooked much of the available evidence and based much of its argument on questionable ethnographic methods.

Indian culture on the eve of European contact is difficult to reconstruct because of the necessity to rely on the writings of European observers. Such sources present formidable problems to the modern interpreter because of their underlying biases, ethnographic ignorance, and the fact that the cultures described had already undergone substantive changes due to the European presence. Failure to account for these limitations—especially the last—has effectively limited the usefulness of many surveys of native culture such as those by Rainey [171], Flannery [80], and Marten [128], as well as such specialized studies as Frank G. Speck's *Territorial Subdivisions and Boundaries of the Wampanoag, Massachusett, and Nauset Indians* [215]. A highly uneven study is Howard S. Russell, *Indian New England Before the Mayflower* [182], which is very informative on material culture and subsistence but fails to distinguish adequately the changes that resulted from contact in such areas as political organization, land tenure, and "tribal" distribution. These problems have generally been more carefully accounted for in the *Handbook* essays noted above. As with other aspects of New England Indian history, these essays are the starting points for the study of pre-contact cultures.

Because southern New England subsistence, especially agriculture, remained essentially unchanged during most of the seventeenth century, it is well documented and has been studied most extensively. Peter Thomas, "Contrastive Subsistence Strategies and Land Use as Factors for Understanding Indian-White Relations in New England" [231], provides an excellent description of those aspects of the native economy. Eva L. Butler illustrated the many dimensions and ramifications of maize cultivation in her "Algonkian Culture and Use of Maize in Southern New England [30], and M. K. Bennett, "The Food Economy of the New England Indians, 1605–75" [14], demonstrates the primacy of domesticated plants in the Indian diet. Frederic W. Warner uses archaeological site reports to provide additional data in "The Foods of the Connecticut Indians" [242]. The role of fire in Indian subsistence strategies is documented and analyzed with great precision in Gordon M. Day, "The Indian as an Ecological Factor in the Northeastern Forest" [54], and more briefly in Calvin Martin, "Fire and Forest Structure in the Aboriginal Eastern Forest" [129]. In "Fish Fertilizer: A Native North American Practice?" [35], Lynn Ceci repudiates a staple of American folklore by answering in the negative, concluding that the Indian, Squanto, must have learned the practice from English settlers in Newfoundland and then taught it to those at Plymouth. While establishing without a doubt that fish fertilizer was not practiced by most agricultural Indians in North America and even New England, Ceci's hypothesis of a Newfoundland origin leaves many questions unanswered. In "Watchers of the Pleiades" [37], Ceci establishes the importance of astronomical observation in determining the timing of the growing season in New England and elsewhere in the northeast.

Among the Abenaki of northern New England, the question of pre-contact subsistence is a sensitive one because of the long-standing debate over whether "family hunting territories" among non-horticultural Algonquians were pre-contact in origin or represented adaptations to the European fur trade. In "Wabanaki 'Family Hunting Territories'" [206], Dean Snow argues that while such an adaptation was made by many northern Algonquian groups, the Abenaki and other Eastern Algonquian hunters had maintained family hunting territories before the arrival of Europeans.

Few other areas of pre-contact culture have received similarly detailed, competent treatment. A lone exception is William S. Simmons, "Southern New England Shamanism" [198]. Simmons has a rare ability to distinguish subjective prejudices from ethnographic realities in the writings of the Puritans and other European observers. The result is a superb overview of a spiritual universe and belief system to the extent that these are revealed in the sources. It should be supplemented by his *Cautantowwit's House* [197], a remarkable archaeological-ethnohistorical study of Narragansett death practices.

A brief but suggestive essay by Robert Steven Grumet, "Sunksquaws, Shamans, and Tradeswomen" [88], treats the generally neglected subject of native women among coastal Algonkian horticulturists. Grumet shows that women played prominent political, economic, and religious-medical roles in their societies both before and after contact, and that the sexual division of labor in those societies was far less pronounced than is usually assumed.

Pre-Settlement Contacts, 1500–1620

History in the United States traditionally com-
mences from an Anglo-philic perspective with the establishment of the first English settlement at James-
town in 1607 or, in the case of New England, with the
landing of the *Mayflower* in 1620. But the closing of the
gap between "history" and "prehistory" is changing all
that. The impact of early, pre-settlement contacts, particularly trade relations and epidemic diseases, is beginning to be understood as the missing link not only
in Indian history but in colonial history. These developments have been sketched for the northeast as a
whole in Brasser, "Early Indian-European Contacts"
[25].

In *Manitou and Providence* [188], and "Squanto:
Last of the Patuxets" [187], Salisbury has focused on
these contacts as the prelude to English settlement. Re-
ferring to coastal New York, including Long Island,
Lynn Ceci has put forth the most provocative argument yet for the importance of a missing link. In her
dissertation, "The Effect of European Contact and
Trade on the Settlement Pattern of Indians in Coastal
New York, 1524–1665: The Archeological and Documentary Evidence" [36], and in "Maize Cultivation in
Coastal New York" [39], Ceci argues that early trade
relations produced many of the cultural patterns often
assumed to be aboriginal, especially year-round coastal
villages and primary dependence on cultivated maize
as a source of food. While Ceci has made a major con-

tribution to our revised understanding of early relations, her overlooking of the possibility that Long
Island, like the New England mainland, was severely
depopulated through epidemic diseases leaves a major
gap in her argument.

In "English-Indian Contacts in New England" [55],
Gordon M. Day considers the gap in the ethnographic
record arising from the poor documentation of this
period. Two additional studies that focus on the European side of these contacts are invaluable both for the
background and details they provide and because their
authors are aware of the ethnohistorical implications of
their subject. David B. Quinn, *North America from Earliest Discovery to First Settlements* [170], devotes portions
or all of several chapters to New England. His is without peer as the definitive work on the history of
Europe's gradual "discovery" of the region and of the
continent as a whole. Douglas R. McManis, *European
Impressions of the New England Coast, 1497–1620* [138],
traces the emergence in maps and documents of an
image of New England—its land and its native
peoples—as a field for European exploitation.

With the exception of Verrazzano's voyage, in
Wroth [257], Indian-European contacts were irregular
and poorly recorded before 1600. The beginnings of
more intensive European activity after that date are a
different story. Most of the sources pertaining to
French and English relations with the natives of New
England's east coast are conveniently assembled in
Charles Herbert Levermore, ed., *Forerunners and Com-*

petitors of the Pilgrims and Puritans [121], though the definitive editions should be consulted for those by Samuel de Champlain [40], Marc Lescarbot [120], Pierre Biard, in the first four volumes of the *Jesuit Relations* [233], and John Smith [204].

The major sources pertaining to Dutch activity on the south coast are included in J. Franklin Jameson, ed., *Narratives of New Netherland, 1609–1664* [98]. A few studies have focused on aspects of Abenaki-French relations. Though he misrepresents Abenaki political organization, Alvin H. Morrison, in "Membertou's Raid on the Chouacoet 'Almouchiquois'—The Micmac Sack of Saco in 1607" [145], documents the participation of the Micmac Indians in France's expansion from Acadia into New England. Lucien Campeau, "La première mission des Jésuites en Nouvelle-France (1611–1613)" [32], provides a thorough account of Biard's effective but short-lived missionary efforts. And Dean Snow, "Abenaki Fur Trade in the Sixteenth Century" [207], explores the impact of intensified contacts in undermining Indian health and autonomy.

This early phase of European activity came to an abrupt end with the plague epidemic of 1616–18 which carried away about 90 percent of the coastal dwelling Indians between the Penobscot River and the eastern shore of Narragansett Bay. The most thorough account from both a medical and a demographic standpoint, though not faultless in the latter, is included in Sherburne F. Cook, "The Significance of Disease in the Extinction of the New England Indians"

[49]. Alfred W. Crosby, "God . . . Would Destroy Them, and Give Their Country to Another People . . ." [52], provides additional insights but offers an explanation of the native interpretation of the epidemic that overlooks much of the relevant evidence.

The Decline of Indian Autonomy: The Colonial Period

White New England's preoccupation with its origins, plus the traditional bias of historians toward significant "turning points," has meant that a disproportionate amount of the scholarship pertaining to native peoples concerns the colonial period. Still, it can be argued that this period was the one in which native cultures changed most radically and the one in which Indians had the greatest impact on non-Indians. Thus the rise of a more systematic "ethnohistorical" approach, combining the methods and findings of archaeology, ethnology, history, and other disciplines, has had little overall effect on the distribution of scholarly efforts. That this is so can be seen by comparing William Fenton's call [77], nearly a quarter of a century ago, with James Axtell's recent progress report, "The Ethnohistory of Early America: A Review Essay" [7]. Whereas Fenton made some modest suggestions as to how such interdisciplinary research might be undertaken, Axtell reviews several major monographs that attest to ethnohistory's rise to academic respectability.

Though Axtell concludes with a long list of topics still to be fully explored, it is a far more specific list than Fenton's and, in virtually all cases, one on which scholars in some areas have begun to act. Taken together, the two essays chart the progress of colonial "ethnohistoriography" and indicate quite clearly that the quantity and quality of scholarship here far exceeds that for all other periods combined.

The arrival of ethnohistory is most apparent in the success of Gary Nash's colonial history text survey, *Red, White, and Black* [153], a revised edition of which is currently being prepared. Nash views colonial America in terms of social and cultural history, focusing not only on factors contributing to white hegemony but on the adaptations by members of all three groups to a rapidly changing world for which their past experiences had provided few precedents. Because of the vastness of his subject, Nash's account is necessarily spotty and brief; his treatment of New England is largely confined to the southern portion through 1676. Yet these sections provide some sharp insights into Indian-settler relations and enable the reader to view those relations alongside those in New France and in the other coastal colonies where subjugation of the natives came early. In this case and in general, Nash has provided an excellent framework for Indian history up to the outbreak of the American Revolution within which events in New England can be placed.

A more specialized study of Indian-English relations is Alden T. Vaughan and Daniel K. Richter,

"Crossing the Cultural Divide" [240] which attempts to quantify instances of individuals passing totally from one culture to the other. The authors conclude that few individuals made such a total transition though many made partial ones, and they are especially effective in demonstrating statistically that few captive colonists "went Indian." But without a rigorous definition of "culture" and without discussions of the two groups' cultural baselines, the article contributes little beyond this statistical corrective.

Though most work on Indians in colonial New England is geographically and chronologically restricted, a few historians have tried for a more general sweep. Douglas Edward Leach's *The Northern Colonial Frontier, 1607–1763* [117], less than a decade older than Nash's, employs a far more traditional approach. While he pays much attention and even sympathy to Indians, Leach makes little effective use of ethnohistorical scholarship. As befits a writer in a series shaped by Frederick Jackson Turner's frontier thesis, he is more interested in the lives of the "pioneers" and in the British-French imperial rivalry. Nevertheless his study includes a good deal of well-documented detail and provides an overview of Indian-European relations in New England and the northeast. Herbert Milton Sylvester's three-volume *Indian Wars of New England* [225] likewise spans the entire period and region. Like many historians of the nineteenth and early twentieth centuries, Sylvester saw Indian-White relations as a tragic, irreconcilable conflict between cruel Whites and "savage" Indians. Though critical of the colonists' morality, Sylvester was not always as critical of their accounts so that not only his moral and ethnographic judgments but many of his factual assertions must be dismissed. Nevertheless he provided useful narrative outlines of the principal military conflicts. A similar assessment can be made of another product of the Victorian era, Samuel G. Drake's *Biography and History of the Indians of North America* [67]. Though less than half of this compendium is concerned with New England, the book is most valuable for the wealth of biographical details on individual Indians of the colonial period. In this respect, it is unmatched. But as with Sylvester, Drake passed on a great deal of colonial "lore" without subjecting it to sufficient critical scrutiny. Today his book serves as a useful reference point for closer study rather than as an authority. Several volumes of Francis Parkman's monumental *France and England in North America* [161] [162] [163] [164] [165] cover aspects of Indian-European relations in New England. Aside from a romantic style which some readers still—a century later—find entertaining, their chief value is in orienting the beginner chronologically and geographically. As colonial history and, particularly, as Indian ethnohistory, they are unreliable. Like Parkman's volumes, those of John Gordon Palfrey, *History of New England* [160], have the virtue, not emulated by any general history written in the twentieth century, of thoroughly integrating Indians into its narrative. But Palfrey unquestioningly followed the historians who wrote officially or quasi-officially for the colonies, so that his work lacks the critical perspective required by students of Indian history.

The nineteenth century witnessed the preservation and publication of much of the colonial documentary record. While many of these works are cited individually in the pages that follow, researchers should peruse the serialized collections of New England's state historical societies, especially for Maine, Massachusetts, and Rhode Island, and the colonial records of Massachusetts Bay [195], Connecticut [237], Rhode Island [12], and Plymouth [196]. The Plymouth records also include those of the Commissioners of the United Colonies of New England, also known as the New England Confederation. Among the hundreds of histories of New England localities, a few are of particular value for students of Indian history, including those by Charles Edward Banks of Martha's Vineyard [11], Frances M. Caulkins of New London and Norwich, Connecticut [34] [33], Frederick Freeman of Cape Cod [82], Alonzo Lewis and James R. Newhall of Lynn, Massachusetts [122], George Sheldon of Deerfield, Massachusetts [193], Alexander Starbuck of Nantucket [220], Josiah Temple of North Brookfield, Massachusetts [228], and Temple and Sheldon of Northfield, Massachusetts [229].

The Subjugation of the Southern Bands

The densely populated agricultural peoples of southern New England were the first to experience the impact of English settlement. During the century and a half following the epidemic of the late 1610s, a rapidly burgeoning English population, hungry for land and righteousness, employed diplomatic, military, missionary, and legal means to gain control of the region from its native inhabitants. To deal with a world in which the balance of numbers and technology steadily grew to their disadvantage, Indian groups employed varying combinations of resistance and accommodation. Some initially undertook a policy of opposition to all things English; others tried to gain maximum advantage by allying themselves with one sector of the English community only; all were subjected in the end to colonial law and converted to some form of Protestant Christianity. Yet these varying approaches were dictated not by the degree of a group's cultural integrity but by external circumstances; the goal in each case was the preservation of Indian communities and identity. This theme is pursued in William John Burton, "Hellish Fiends and Brutish Men" [28], a suggestive dissertation whose chief virtue is its attention to Indian motives and actions as rooted in a cultural framework. Burton has an unfortunate tendency to be dazzled by anthropological models that only superficially represent ethnohistorical realities, especially native political organization. There are also many gaps in his account, especially with regard to demography and epidemiology. Still, this is an excellent place to become acquainted with the history of cultural interaction in broad outline. It can be supplemented by Lorraine E. Williams, "Ft. Shantok

and Ft. Corchaug" [249], an archaeological-
ethnohistorical study which indicates the extent to
which native cultural change can be measured by material remains. Williams finds that while the Corchaug
of eastern Long Island were under conditions of "directed" contact by 1640, the Mohegan of southern
Connecticut postponed this extreme until the 1680s.
For the Indian impact on English culture, on the other
hand, see James Axtell, "The Scholastic Philosophy of
the Wilderness" and "The Indian Impact on English
Colonial Culture," two essays in his *The European and the
Indian* [8]. Though countless studies of this subject
have been produced, Axtell is the only author to con-
sider the role of actual Indians and their culture,
rather than purely subjective images, as shaping
influences on settler values and behavior.

One of the major gaps in Burton's presentation can
be filled by a reading of Sherburne F. Cook, "The
Significance of Disease in the Extinction of the New
England Indians" [49], which documents epidemic and
endemic diseases and considers their impact on Indian
mortality and morale. Cook underestimates pre-contact
population, some of his sources are of questionable
authority, and many of his estimates are so general as
to be no more than vague guesses. But his study convincingly demonstrates that disease was far and away
the chief source of the massive depopulation of Indians
throughout the colonial period.

Most of the scholarly attention in recent years has
been paid to the early period of colonization in south-

ern New England, ending with King Philip's War (1675–76), during which overt Indian resistance was effectively squelched. A lively historiographical controversy has been generated, primarily by two general studies with sharply differing views of the period. First published in 1965, Alden T. Vaughan in *New England Frontier* [239], argued that Puritan treatment of the Indians was fair and just, given the cultural propensities of each group. (In a recent revision, Vaughan admits that his original argument was oversimplified in some respects and modifies a few of his more extreme statements, but his position is fundamentally unchanged.) Because of his uncritical acceptance of Puritan accounts and his ignorance of relevant ethnohistory, Vaughan was highly vulnerable to criticism. The extent of that vulnerability can be measured in the flood of works that have appeared subsequently.

The earliest of these, such as Neal Salisbury's "Conquest of the 'Savage'" [185], and James Axtell, "Through a Glass Darkly: Colonial Attitudes Toward the Native Americans" [6], found the colonists culturally and intellectually disposed toward the kind of total conquest that in fact occurred. Then Francis Jennings, in *The Invasion of America* [101], mounted a massive challenge not only to Vaughan but to virtually the entire tradition of historical writing on the subject of Indian-Puritan relations. Jennings argued that this tradition was characterized by an uncritical acceptance of Puritan accounts of themselves as "civilized" and the Indians as "savage," offering instead a revisionist account in which Indians were recognized, for nearly the first time, as human beings with interests of their own rather than as stereotypical "savages," noble or ignoble, in a mythic drama. For Jennings, the Puritan conquest of Indians and their lands was not inevitable but rather the result of deliberate calculation, reinforced by greed and a willingness to employ almost any means available. In a review essay, David C. Stineback, "The Status of Puritan-Indian Scholarship" [222], accused Jennings of erring too far in the opposite direction from Vaughan by discounting the reality of the Puritans' beliefs in Indian "savagery" and underestimating the "theocratic view of reality" that guided their behavior. In *Manitou and Providence* [188], Salisbury views the values and actions of both groups as shaped by their historical experiences—the natives by their deeply rooted cultures plus their pre-colonial contacts with Europeans, the settlers by the economic and religious upheavals of Tudor-early Stuart England.

The best short introduction to the various Indian groups, as well as to the history, of the period is Salwen, "Indians of Southern New England and Long Island: Early Period" [190]. The Narragansett are the subject of three histories written during the nineteenth and early twentieth centuries. Elisha R. Potter, Jr., *The Early History of Narragansett* [168], provides a narrative of events from the beginning of colonization to the early eighteenth century in annalistic form, liberally quoting and paraphrasing earlier authors. Henry C. Dorr, "The Narragansetts" [65], was yet another Victorian who saw Indians as declining in the face of a superior civilization. Both histories are noteworthy for their factual detail and their Rhode Islanders' critical attitude toward the "mainstream" colonies of Massachusetts Bay and Connecticut. Howard M. Chapin, *Sachems of the Narragansetts* [41], focuses on the group's leaders and the institution of the sachemship as the basis for his narrative. Though he erred in seeing native political structures as essentially "feudal," his book conveys the importance of marital alliances among ruling lineages in southern New England and provides an excellent account of Narragansett relations with English and other Indian groups through 1676. The treatment is much briefer thereafter until the abolition of the hereditary sachemship in the late eighteenth century. A similar misreading of Indian political organization only slightly mars the useful overview of Indian-European relations in Plymouth colony by Maurice Robbins, printed as "Indians of the Old Colony" [175]. The relevant sections of Allen W. Trelease, *Indian Affairs in Colonial New York: The Seventeenth Century* [235], are indispensable for following events on New England's western frontier and for understanding relations between the natives, and between the European policies, of these two regions.

A number of literary sources from this period provide excellent insights into native culture as well as Indian-English relations. Though intended as a combined linguistic guide and theological tract, Roger Williams, *A Key into the Language of America* [250], is the best ethnography of the period. Also of particular value are Thomas Morton, *New English Canaan* [151], William Wood, *New England's Prospect* [254], Edward Winslow, *Good News from New England* [253], and John Josselyn, *An Account of Two Voyages to New-England* [105].

Economic exchanges between natives and Europeans in the early colonial period varied greatly depending on the circumstances under which each was conducted. In most cases, regular exchange began with at least a brief period in which Indians traded furs for items of European manufacture. Two general studies of the trade view it from English perspectives but are useful for the information they provide. Francis X. Moloney, *The Fur Trade in New England, 1620–1676* [144], views the traders as preparing the way for English farmers and only notes Indians in passing. William I. Roberts, "The Fur Trade of New England in the Seventeenth Century" [176], on the other hand, focuses on the role of the trade in the colonial economy and looks more closely at the merchants who financed it. He is also more attentive to the role of Indians in the trade and to the trade's impact on native culture. The outstanding study of Indian-English exchanges is Peter Allen Thomas, "In the Maelstrom of Change" [232]. Thomas argues that pre-contact exchanges fulfilled social and political, as well as material, imperatives and that these imperatives explain the Indians' growing dependence on the trade during the course of the seventeenth century. Besides advancing our understanding of Indian trading behavior in general, Thomas has produced the first thorough study of interior southern New England, drawing on the rarely used papers of the Pynchon trading dynasty and undertaking an archaeological analysis of one village site.

One of the staples in the early fur trade was wampum, which Indians fashioned from quahog shells found on the shores of Long Island Sound and traded to inland groups for furs. Historians such as William B. Weeden [244] have traditionally assumed that wampum was a form of money improvised to fill the needs of the fur trade and later of the colonial economy. But J. S. Slotkin and Karl Schmitt, "Studies of Wampum" [203], and Mary W. Herman, "Wampum as a Money in Northeastern North America" [91], indicate that Indians exchanged wampum among themselves for non-economic reasons long before contact with Europeans. Most recently, Lynn Ceci has returned to the earlier view, arguing in "The Effect of European Contact and Trade" [36] and in "The First Fiscal Crisis in New York" [38] that competition for wampum was the principal factor in not only the Indian-European wars of New Netherland and southwestern New England but in Dutch-English conflict up to and including the British takeover of New Netherland in 1664.

Most studies of the exchange of land by Indians are part of the more general works listed earlier, though there are numerous studies of English theories of sovereignty and land ownership that say nothing about actual Indians. Two articles examine land transactions and indicate their economic and political impact on the native sellers. In "Virgin Land and Savage People" [100], Francis Jennings notes that English and Dutch colonists employed legal formalities when they deemed it expedient to do so, usually to beat out a European rival, and that Indians were the losers regardless of the particular course followed. He also points out that the eastern Massachusetts deeds on which the Bay colony's reputation for fairness rests were drawn up long after the fact of sale to buttress the colony's legitimacy. In "The Technique of Seventeenth Century Indian-Land Purchases" [256], Harry Andrew Wright examined some of the purchases made by the Pynchons in the Connecticut River Valley, providing a picture of the disadvantaged position of Indian sellers.

The legal treatment of subject Indians has received little attention aside from Vaughan's argument for colonial fairness. But two articles do offer some basis for questioning that view. James P. Ronda, "Red and White at the Bench" [177], shows that legal subjugation in Plymouth County grew tighter, along with the demographic and economic imbalance favoring the settlers. In a similar vein, Lyle Koehler, "Red-White Power Relations and Justice in the Courts of Seventeenth-Century New England" [113], demonstrates that the harshness of punishments meted out to Indians reflected the security and confidence of the punishing colony vis-à-vis its native inhabitants. Though the arguments and methods of the two authors differ, both show the emergence of discriminatory justice during the seventeenth century. A rare instance of Whites being punished for a major crime against an Indian is the subject of LaFantasie, "Murder of an Indian, 1638" [114].

The role of Puritan missions and missionaries in the larger context of Indian-English relations has been the subject of recent debate among historians. The motives and goals of the missionaries, the responses of various native groups, and the political and cultural effects of the missions have all been assessed with differing results by different scholars. Several surveys, covering the colonial period as a whole, are more concerned with the history of missions than of Indians but nevertheless provide valuable background. William Kellaway, *The New England Company, 1649–1776* [110], is an excellent institutional history which covers the entire operation, including the London-based financial and administrative apparatus. Frederick L. Weis, "The New England Company of 1649 and its Missionary Enterprises" [245] provides a much briefer survey; its real value is its lengthy appendix which lists every known Indian church and praying town and every preacher, native as well as English. Though it contains a few factual errors, Weis's account is a most useful research tool. Margery Ruth Johnson, "The Mayhew Mission to the Indians, 1643–1806" [102], is a comprehensive survey of the Mayhew family's long involvement in Indian religious life on the island of Martha's Vineyard. Johnson has little understanding of Indian cultural change and is thus unable to explain much of the history she records, such as the rise of the Baptist religion among the Indians in the later colonial period. The same can be said of an older study of Indian converts in the New Haven area, Charles Hervey Townshend, "The Quinnipiac Indians and their Reservations" [234]. Two new books offer a far more balanced perspective on the missions and their converts. Henry Warner Bowden, *Native Americans and Christian Missions* [20], a survey of that subject from the colonial period to the present examines New England missions, and James Axtell, *The European and the Indian* [8] includes several essays that pertain to missions by one of the leading ethnohistorians writing on the colonial period. Both authors assess the missions as intercultural encounters in which both successes and failures reveal much about those who participated.

Much of the recent scholarly attention has gone toward the work of John Eliot among the Massachusets and Nipmucks of eastern Massachusetts. In "Goals and Functions of Puritan Missions to the Indians" [99], Francis Jennings argues that Eliot consciously served colonial expansion while in "Red Puritans" [186], Salisbury suggests that Eliot's intent was not so conscious but had the same result. Kenneth M. Morrison, "'That Art of Coyning Christians'" [146], argues along the same lines, stressing the enormous cultural gap separating the two peoples. In "Indian Devils and Pilgrim Fathers" [194], Frank Shuffelton notes the failure of the early Plymouth colonists to understand the deeper meanings of native religion. Though this failure had no adverse consequences at the time, it undoubtedly contributed to the missionaries' limited successes later. The more lasting conversions effected by Thomas Mayhew, working among the Indians of Martha's Vineyard, have been attributed to his less coercive methods by Jennings and by William S. Simmons, "Conversion from Indian to Puritan" [200]. Besides Margery Johnson's dissertation noted above, Mayhew's efforts are thoroughly covered in the biography by Lloyd C.M. Hare, *Thomas Mayhew, Patriarch to the Indians* [90]

Some scholars have recently taken issue with interpretations that seem to stress the passivity of Indian converts in the face of active acculturation efforts by missionaries. So far, such viewpoints have not been the basis for analysis except in James P. Ronda, "'We Are Well as We Are': An Indian Critique of Seventeenth-Century Missions" [178], which examines vocal Indian resistance to the efforts of both the Puritans and of the Jesuits in New France. That mission Indians retained control over critical areas of their lives is evident in Susan L. MacCulloch, "A Tripartite Political System among Christian Indians of Early Massachusetts" [125], which demonstrates how native political structures persisted in the "praying towns" despite Eliot's efforts to undermine them. Literacy in English was another means by which Christian Indians might hope to flourish, albeit in non-traditional fashion. The varying careers of the handful of literate Indians are recorded in Walter T. Meserve, "English Works of Seventeenth-Century Indians" [141].

Because the missionaries depended on English funds to support their operations, they produced a great deal of publicity designed to further that end. Though this material often exaggerated missionary success and native receptivity, it remains valuable for its descriptions of Indian-missionary encounters, Indian conversions, and "praying town" life. The most thorough primary account of missionary activity is Daniel Gookin, "Historical Collections of the Indians in New England [86], which includes a survey of all missionaries and praying towns on the eve of King Philip's War. Most of the missionary accounts were reprinted in a single issue of the *Collections of the Massachusetts Historical Society* [131]. While much of this material is missionary propaganda, it also includes conversion experiences and confessions as given by the Indians themselves. These provide direct insights into native responses to Christianity, as do the fictional conversations presented by Eliot in his *Indian Dialogues* [21], which have been recently edited by Henry W. Bowden and James P. Ronda. Perhaps the most valuable of all sources is Experience Mayhew, *Indian Converts* [135], most of which consists of 126 biographical profiles of three generations of Martha's Vineyard Christian Indians. The profiles include information on the subjects' lives before their conversions, the impact of conversion on families (women tended to convert sooner and more frequently than their husbands), emotional and other factors, such as alcohol, which impeded or facilitated conversion, and a wealth of additional material. As James P. Ronda has demonstrated in "Generations of

Faith" [179], Mayhew's account taken as a whole, shows how Christianity had gradually become integral to native life on the island by the 1720s.

As decisive as were the religious encounters between natives and settlers, it was their military and diplomatic encounters which had a more immediate impact on their lives. A good, brief introduction to the military conflicts and their historiography is Wilcomb E. Washburn, "Seventeenth-Century Wars" [243], which also covers events in Virginia and New Netherland so as to provide a comparative perspective. Much of Washburn's treatment concerns the inevitability of the major wars and the justness of the English cause, issues which have traditionally exercised historians. But ethnohistorians examining the Pequot War (1637) have found traditional accounts to be so deficient in their understanding of Indian history and politics as to render them inadequate. Bert Salwen, "A Tentative 'In Situ' Solution to the Mohegan-Pequot Problem" [189], for example, disputes the notion that the Pequot were recent migrants or invaders on the Connecticut coast who had driven native groups from their homelands. He cites both archaeological and linguistic evidence for their *in situ* origins. His "tentative solution" has since been reinforced and is now accepted as factual. The motives for the Mohegans' siding with the colonists against the Pequots in that war have also come under scrutiny. Carroll Alton Means, "Mohegan-Pequot Relationships" [140], drew on rarely cited post-war native testimony showing that the two groups were not recent

newcomers and that what united them politically were
nothing more than marriages between members of
sachem lineages. But Means was apparently reluctant
to break decisively with traditional accounts and so
concluded that the Mohegan had been "subordinate"
to the Pequot until Uncas led their "secession." This
conclusion was echoed in even less successful articles by
Metcalf, "Who Should Rule at Home?" [142] and by
Burton and Lowenthal, "The First of the Mohegans"
[29], which applied anthropological models to the
problem but failed to investigate the historical context
as thoroughly as Means had. The Pequot War itself has
been studied most closely in the general histories of
early Indian-English relations cited earlier. There are
no primary accounts that give much indication of the
Pequots' perspective on the conflict. The four major
English accounts, useful if regarded critically, are conveniently assembled in Charles Orr, ed., *History of the
Pequot War* [158].

After the war, the four mainstream Puritan
colonies—Massachusetts Bay, Connecticut, Plymouth,
and New Haven—directed their hostilities toward the
powerful Narragansets and their Niantic allies, backed
only by tiny, renegade Rhode Island. In 1643 these
colonies formalized their relationship in the United
Colonies of New England, whose first act was to order
the assassination of the Narraganset sachem, Miantonomi, by their leading Indian ally, Uncas of the
Mohegans. This action, and the background of events
leading up to it, is recounted in John A. Sainsbury,

"Miantonomo's Death and New England Politics, 1630–1645" [183]. Though weak for the pre-Pequot period, Sainsbury is more thorough and reliable thereafter. William L. Stone, *Uncas and Miantonomoh* [223], is a nineteenth-century, pro-Puritan account that is little more than an apology for the former and a blanket condemnation of the latter. Following Miantonomi's death, the leading figure in the alliance was Ninigret of the Niantic. This little-understood sachem is the subject of a useful essay by Timothy S. Sehr, "Ninigret's Tactics of Accommodation" [191], which stresses his active role in attempting to come to terms with the reality of English colonization without compromising his own people's cultural and political integrity.

The decisive conflict was King Philip's War (1675–76), the conclusion of which serves as the major divide in colonial Indian history. The leading study of the war, Douglas Edward Leach, *Flintlock and Tomahawk* [116], is a solid narrative account but should be supplemented by Jennings, *Invasion of America* [101], for a more critical view of the English sources. An older study, George W. Ellis and John E. Morris, *King Philip's War* [75] is subject to the same criticism as Leach. The difficulties in penetrating the English sources are apparent in a bit of detective work applied to one of the war's "triggering incidents" by James P. Ronda and Jeanne Ronda, "The Death of John Sassamon" [180]. Of the sources themselves, the most useful are those based on direct contact with Indians. Despite its virulently anti-Indian bias, Mary Rowlandson's famous captivity narrative, in Lincoln [123], provides a first-hand look at anti-English Indians during wartime. Benjamin Church, *The History of King Philip's War* [43], on the other hand, describes personal relationships between natives and settlers on the eastern shore of Narragansett Bay, where the conflict erupted, and his effective use of Indians to fight other Indians. Daniel Gookin provided "An Historical Account of the Doings and Sufferings of the Christian Indians in New England" [87] that documents both the services rendered and the atrocities suffered by the converts who supported the colonial cause. Of the formal Puritan histories of the war, William Hubbard, *The Present State of New-England* [94], is far more detailed and useful than Increase Mather, *A Brief History of the War with the Indians in New-England* [132], and the same author's *A Relation of the Troubles which Have happened in New-England* [133], which covers the Pequot War and inter-war period as well. But both should be used with extreme caution as should the additional English accounts in Charles Lincoln, ed., *Narratives of the Indian Wars* [123]. Besides Rowlandson's narrative, the latter collection is especially valuable for the account by John Easton, a Rhode Island Quaker, of the war's beginnings.

A major factor in the English victories was their military technology. Yet, as Patrick M. Malone has shown [127], Indians adapted to this technology far more quickly than the English adapted their fighting methods to New England conditions. But while using and repairing flintlocks with ease, the natives were never able to produce, or to procure a steadily reliable source of gunpowder to operate them.

The cumulative impact of the wars, ending as they did with King Philip's, was devastating for the natives. In "Interracial Warfare and Population Decline Among the New England Indians" [48], Sherburne F. Cook estimates that their numbers decreased by about one fourth as a result. A portion of this decline is attributable to emigration, much of it involuntary. Many Indians captured by the English in the Pequot and King Philip's Wars were enslaved and sold abroad as punishment for resisting the English. The laws and practices surrounding Indian slavery were examined exhaustively at the beginning of this century in Almon Wheeler Lauber, *Indian Slavery in Colonial Times* [115]. Lauber's evidence indicates that southern New England was second only to the notorious Carolinas in the numbers of Indians enslaved. The fates of most overseas slaves is unknown but in "Bermuda's Pequots" [130], Van Wyck Mason traced one group which, while adapting to life in Bermuda, retained its Pequot identity into this century.

The lot of the colonists' native allies after the war was hardly any better. They shared not only disease and impoverishment with the "hostiles" but with them were subjected to restrictive and discriminatory legislation that relegated them to lower-caste status. The decline of the Indians' political and legal position over the next century in Massachusetts is effectively charted in a series of articles by Yasu Kawashima. In "Jurisdiction

of the Colonial Courts over the Indians in Massachusetts, 1689–1763" [106], Kawashima notes that the
legal standings of Indians differed, depending on
whether they were members of frontier tribes, of
"plantations" (reservations), or were unattached individuals. Here, and more thoroughly in "Legal Origins
of the Indian Reservation in Colonial Massachusetts"
[107], he demonstrates how the reservations grew out
of the earlier praying towns and how the native resi-
dents' autonomy in these towns continued to decline
through the eighteenth century. And in "Forced Conformity" [108], Kawashima discovers that while Indians
were generally regarded equally with Whites, they
came in for especially prompt and harsh punishment
when convicted of crimes perpetrated against Whites
or in white settlements. As he suggests, this discrepancy
reveals an underlying bias that further reinforced the
tendencies toward racial segregation in late colonial
New England.

The decline of Indian autonomy in what had been
John Eliot's model praying town is traced in Michael J.
Crawford, "Indians, Yankees, and the Meetinghouse
Dispute of Natick, Massachusetts, 1743–1800" [51].
Though Crawford is primarily interested in the White
settlers and pays little attention to Indian viewpoints
and motives, his narrative indicates how demographic
and economic factors plus political and legal discrimination worked to bring about the demise of one Indian
community. Crawford's account can be supplemented
by that of Stephen Badger, the white minister who was

sympathetic toward, if not entirely understanding of, the Indians' situation [9]. A somewhat different kind of encroachment on traditionally friendly Indians occurred with the Mohegan in Connecticut. The tangled history of this tribe's long-standing and finally unsuccessful, legal effort to retain its land holdings has been ably presented by Joseph Henry Smith in a section of his *Appeals to the Privy Council from the American Plantations* [205].

Another dimension of economic decline among Indians was occupational. With their land bases reduced and their freedom of movement restricted, natives in eighteenth-century southern New England increasingly ended up on the pauper rolls. As John A. Sainsbury points out in "Indian Labor in Early Rhode Island" [184], the dependent poor among the Narragansets and Niantics were often bound out as servants and—despite legislation prohibiting it—as slaves. For Indian males who were not bound, one source of income was as soldiers in New England's wars with the French and Abenakis to the north. Richard R. Johnson, in "The Search for a Usable Indian" [103], has examined this phenomenon through the first quarter of the eighteenth century, focusing principally on its significance for the colonists' self-image. As in King Philip's War, Indian troops were especially effective against other Indians. And as in that war, their most effective commander was Benjamin Church, who recounted his exploits and frustrations, and those of his men, in a second volume of memoirs, *The History of the Eastern Expeditions* [44].

Though little work on the everyday life of Indians in this period has yet been done, two recent research notes suggest some dimensions of that life. Kathleen J. Bragdon, using "Probate Records as a Source for Algonquian Ethnohistory" [22], shows several ways that the lives of Indians in this period can be documented and compared to those of their ancestors and of non-Indians in their own time. William C. Sturtevant, "Two 1761 Wigwams at Niantic, Connecticut" [224], indicates the way a traditional house type with a wide distribution in North America continued to be used in eighteenth-century southern New England, at least during summers. Continuity in a variety of customs was also reflected in the brief "Account of the Montauk Indians" [156], written by the Mohegan preacher, Samson Occom, in 1761.

The devastation wrought by King Philip's War extended to the "praying Indians." Rawson and Danforth's brief and incomplete survey [172] of Christian Indians in Massachusetts at the end of the century provides a dismal contrast to the prewar figures given by Eliot and Gookin. For more than half a century after the war, missionary efforts in southern New England were essentially holding actions in which ministers, both native and white, attempted to keep the faith alive in communities where it was already established. Experience Mayhew, *Indian Converts* [135], details the results of such efforts in the native villages of Martha's Vineyard. Occasional missionary efforts among the unconverted met with indifference and, on occasion, overt opposition. These were the reactions Mayhew encountered in 1713 and 1714 when he journeyed among the major non-converted groups of Rhode Island and Connecticut. Mayhew's journals of these expeditions are included in the collection of missionary correspondence edited by John W. Ford [81].

The first break in the missionary impasse came not among Indians living in the older areas of English settlement but on southern New England's last frontier, the Berkshire mountains. Here the English population began to increase markedly during the second quarter of the eighteenth century, crowding not only the natives of the region but those Indians who had sought refuge there after being driven from their homes in southeastern New England and lower New York. John Sergeant began preaching in one such community in 1734. The Stockbridge mission, as it was called, quickly became a success despite opposition from some natives. Besides the establishment of a church, a town government was formed, land was allotted to individuals for farming, and a boarding school for Indian boys and girls was begun. Yet according to Hendrick Aupaumut, a later leader of the community whose "History of the Muhheakunnuk Indians" is included in Electa F. Jones, *Stockbridge, Past and Present* [104], these accoutrements of "civilization" marked no simple break from the converts' native pasts. Rather they represented a synthesis of Indian and English traditions with Christianity as its keystone and excluding the more destructive elements of the two cultures. Besides Aupaumut and Jones, Samuel Hopkins, *Historical Memoirs, Relating to the*

Housatunnuk Indians [93], is a good account that is highly favorable to Sergeant and follows Stockbridge through his death in 1749. A second effort in the Berkshires was undertaken by Moravians working in northwestern Connecticut and across the line in New York during the early 1740s. These efforts also enjoyed success from the outset but were opposed and, eventually, ended by the English settlers and governments who accused the Moravians of turning the Indians against the British Crown. The story is told most succinctly and ably in the later chapters of Orcutt, *The Indians of the Housatonic and Naugatuck Valleys* [157], an excellent introduction to colonial Indian-White relations in western Connecticut.

Christianity arrived among the remaining Indians quite suddenly as part of the general rise of pietistic revivalism in the American colonies known as the Great Awakening. In southern New England, this movement represented a popular rejection of the more intellectual approach to religion that hitherto had dominated Puritan churches, including the Indian missions. As William S. Simmons points out in "The Great Awakening and Indian Conversion" [201], the Narragansett and other hitherto unconverted groups found in this new variant of Calvinism a faith that was compatible with their cultural traditions on one hand and their ideological needs for the future on the other. The awakening inspired a number of white preachers to work among the Indians as missionaries, the most ambitious of whom was Eleazar Wheelock. Like Sergeant,

he established a boarding school for Indian
Children—Moor's Charity School. James Dow McCallum has written a thorough but racially biased biography of Wheelock [136], and has edited a remarkable
source collection, *The Letters of Eleazar Wheelock's Indians.* [137]. The letters show the inter-cultural tensions
to which the Moor's students were subjected as well as
the adaptive role Christianity played for some. In "Dr.
Wheelock's Little Red School," an essay in his *The European and the Indian* [8], James Axtell analyzes
Wheelock's failure to educate the Indians and his shift
to the collegiate education of white ministers. Margaret
Connell Szasz, "'Poor Richard' Meets the Native American: Schooling for Young Indian Women in
Eighteenth-Century Connecticut" [226], demonstrates
the strength and persistence of traditional culture
among these students, male as well as female.

The most famous of all Wheelock's pupils was
Samson Occom, the Mohegan who became a Christian
preacher and, in later years, a Christian nationalist
leader disillusioned with his mentor. Harold Blodgett
has written a good biography, *Samson Occom* [15].
Occom gained international fame when he toured England in the late 1760s to raise funds for Wheelock's
Indian school. The many sources relating to this jour-
ney and to Occom's break with Wheelock have been
collected and edited by Leon Burr Richardson in *An
Indian Preacher in England* [173].

The Northern Frontier

Whereas the agricultural bands of southern New England were confronted from the beginning by the presence of an English settler population, the colonial history of the native peoples of northern New England followed a markedly different course. Located on the frontier between New England and New France, the various Abenaki-speaking groups experienced an even more complicated set of pressures: from the south, a dependence on trade with the English plus increasing numbers of land-hungry settlers; from the north, the religious and military support offered by Jesuit missionaries and French officials; and from the west, the necessity of reckoning with the imposing presence of the League of the Iroquois. In the end, the region was conquered by English colonists — not solely, as in southern New England, because of inexorable settler expansion into their homeland but as the outcome of British-French imperial rivalry in North America as a whole. No single-volume overview of Abenaki colonial history has been written but a good starting point is the dissertation by Kenneth M. Morrison, "The People of the Dawn" [148], a brilliant demonstration of how the Eastern Abenaki were guided by their own values and interests through the mazeway of international politics. Morrison's chronological account can be supplanted by the topical analysis of Alfred Goldsworthy Bailey, *The Conflict of European and Eastern Algonkian Cultures* [10], which tends to place more emphasis on native decline.

Unfortunately, both studies do not extend much beyond the beginning of the eighteenth century in their coverage.

Though focused on the natives of eastern Canada, Bailey also gives attention to the Abenakis, both in Maine and in the Jesuit-run villages of Quebec to which many of them fled. This is in contrast to other Canadian histories of the Abenakis, such as the useful nineteenth-century account by Joseph Maurault, *Histoire des Abénakis* [134] and the recent, largely unsuccessful attempt to unravel Abenaki nomenclature by P.-André Sévigny, *Les Abénaquis* [192], which overlook those who remained in Maine. The history of the Western Abenakis (those from the upper Merrimack River westward) before and after emigration was badly misunderstood until Gordon M. Day began publishing his findings less than a quarter of a century ago. Combining linguistic expertise, historical precision, and ethnographic sensitivity, Day has documented "The Indian Occupation of Vermont" [57] in a region once thought to have been populated by few if any Indians; and demonstrated that the eastern shore of Lake Champlain was the original home for some Abenakis, in "The Eastern Boundary of Iroquoia" [59], and, later, for refugees from many war-torn villages in New England and the Hudson Valley in "Missisquoi" [60]. Day has also established "The Identity of the Sokokis" [56] as the "Squawheag" of English accounts who lived on the Connecticut River near present Northfield, Massachusetts, and not the Indians of the Saco River in

Maine. Our knowledge of this group's history in the
seventeenth century has been further expanded by
Peter Allen Thomas who reports his archaeological and
documentary findings in "Squakheag Ethnohistory"
[230]. The history of St. Francis, the largest community
of New England Indian refugees, including virtually all
of the Western Abenakis, is the subject of a thorough
history by Thomas-M. Charland, *Histoire des Abénakis
d'Odanak* [42].

The history of missionary efforts among the
Abenakis who remained in Maine has been effectively
chronicled by Sister Mary Celeste Leger, in *The Catholic
Indian Missions in Maine* [118]. The Jesuits of New
France, including the two major figures in Maine—
Gabriel Druillettes and Sébastien Râle—are the subjects of two provocative essays which conclude that the
missionaries were fully integrated, socially and ideolog-
ically, into their converts' communities. Robert Conkling, "Legitimacy and Conversion in Social Change:
The Case of French Missionaries and the Northeastern
Algonkian" [47], argues that the Abenakis accorded the
Jesuits shamanistic powers to counter the destruction
wrought by European colonization. Kenneth M. Morrison, "Toward a History of Intimate Encounters" [149],
emphasizes the interpersonal dimension of Jesuit-
convert relations and draws on oral traditions collected
in the nineteenth century to suggest that the missionaries also assumed the mythological roles of
Abenaki culture heroes.

Native traditions are likewise a principal source for

our knowledge of the Wabanaki Confederacy, fashioned by the Eastern Abenakis along with the Passamaquoddys, the Malecites, and the Micmacs during the eighteenth century. As Willard Walker, et al., point out in "A Chronological Account of the Wabanaki Confederacy" [241], missionaries helped shape the Confederacy's politics by gaining influence in the large inter-band councils traditionally held among northeastern Algonquians. In "The Eastern Algonkian Wabanaki Confederacy" [211], Frank G. Speck notes that the Confederacy was influenced in many of its forms by the League of the Iroquois as well as having developed, in part, as a counterweight to the League. Speck also noted the many ceremonial usages of wampum in Confederacy protocol and rituals in "The Functions of Wampum among the Eastern Algonkian" [212]. The Passamaquoddys' traditions regarding the Confederacy's origins and its principal rituals were recorded and translated by John Dyneley Prince in his *Passamaquoddy Texts* [169].

Gabriel Druillettes represented the only important source of French influence among the Abenakis during the middle decades of the seventeenth century. His own account of his relations with the Kennebec Abenakis and his diplomatic endeavors among the New England colonies are included in volume 36 of the *Jesuit Relations* [233]. Good accounts by other Jesuits can be found in volumes 31 and 38. A useful narrative of events, but one that sheds little light on the Abenaki converts themselves, is John Marshall Brown, "The

Mission of the Assumption on the River Kennebec, 1646–1652" [27].

The courting of the Abenakis by the French remained sporadic until 1670 when the latter fortified Pentagoet at the mouth of the Penobscot River. In 1674, a young French officer, the Baron de St.-Castin, reinforced the two peoples' ties by taking up residence among the Penobscot Abenakis and marrying the daughter of the powerful sagamore, Madockawando. The subject of much literary romanticizing in the nineteenth century, St.-Castin deserves the kind of scrutiny for his impact on the Abenakis that has been recently accorded the missionaries. A good foundation for such an effort is in the biography by Pierre Daviault, *Le Baron de Saint-Castin, Chef Abénaquis* [53], and the review of his life by Graham Munson, "St. Castin: A Legend Revised" [152], which show the difficulties the Abenakis faced as they struggled to maintain their cultural and political autonomy while living between two imperial powers.

This struggle remained central for the Abenakis despite the fact that in the wars that ensued most of them sided with the French. For general histories of these conflicts, the reader must rely on older accounts, usually biased toward the English and against the Abenakis. (An exception is Kenneth M. Morrison's excellent essay on King Philip's War in Maine, "The Bias of Colonial Law" [150], which sees the war's cause in the unrestrained violence of English frontier settlers and the two peoples' radically different legal cultures.)

The second and third volumes of Sylvester, *Indian Wars of New England* [225] cover the major wars between 1675 and 1762. Two of these, "King William's" (1689–97) and "Queen Anne's" (1702–13), are detailed in Samuel Adams Drake, *The Border Wars of New England* [66], and a third, "Governor Shirley's" (1744–49), is recounted by that author's father, Samuel G. Drake, in *A Particular History of the Five Years French and Indian War in New England* [68]. A classic Puritan account of Indian-English conflict during the first quarter of the eighteenth century, with all the deficiencies of its genre, is Samuel Penhallow, *The History of the Wars of New-England With the Eastern Indians* [166]. More direct English perspectives can be obtained from some of the numerous accounts by persons captured by Indians and French. Of these the most factually informative are by John Gyles, included in Samuel G. Drake, ed., *Indian Captivities* [69], and John Williams [248]. Though it contains a number of errors and exaggerations, Horace P. Beck, *The American Indian as a Sea-Fighter in Colonial Times* [13] documents the extensive maritime warfare of the eastern Abenakis (along with the Malecites and Micmacs of eastern Canada) in which they used shallops and other European boats as well as their own canoes.

In 1694, while St.-Castin was still established on the Penobscot, Sebastian Râle began his mission at the village of Norridgewock on the Kennebec. The mission flourished until it was destroyed in an English attack in 1724, part of the conflict known variously as Lovewell's, Râle's, and, most appropriately, Dummer's

War (1722–25). Râle's letters, and other Jesuit documents pertaining to his mission are collected in volume 67 of the *Jesuit Relations* [233]. Fanny Hardy Eckstorm, in "The Attack on Norridgewock, 1724" [71], argues that a number of letters establishing Râle's reputation as a saintly martyr are forgeries and that, in truth, he was opposed by many of the Norridgewocks as a despotic ruler and French agent. Kenneth M. Morrison, "Sebastian Racle and Norridgewock, 1724" [147], has responded directly to Eckstorm, contending that the letters were genuine and that Râle was accepted as a benevolent presence by virtually all the Norridgewocks. Eckstorm has more convincingly probed the battle celebrated as "Lovewell's Fight" (1725), pointing to distortions in the English sources arising from a desire to protect an English participant's posthumous reputation, in "Pigwacket and Parson Symmes" [72], and to the subsequent romanticization of one of the natives who died there, in "Who Was Paugus?" [73]. Many insights into Abenaki grievances against the English during this period can be gained from the transcripts of the four treaty conferences included in "Indian Treaties" [97]. The twenty-four volume *Documentary History of the State of Maine* [126] is a vast compendium of sources on Abenaki-English relations during this period.

Indians and America's Revolution

The withdrawal of the French served only to heighten tensions in northern New England between the natives and the English intruders who hunted and squatted on their lands and traded dishonestly with them. B. J. Whiting has reported on one such set of tensions involving the Penobscot Abenaki, English hunters and land speculators, and the Massachusetts government that resulted in an "Incident at Quantabacook, March, 1764" [247]. Meanwhile, the Western Abenakis remained relatively free of such pressures until the outbreak of the War for Independence. This is clear from the first-person account of a colonist who lived with one group of them from 1772 to 1775, as discussed in Gordon M. Day, "Henry Tufts as a Source on the Eighteenth Century Abenakis" [61].

As Walker, et al. [241], make clear, most members of the Wabanaki Confederacy supported the Patriots militarily because the latter were, like themselves, allied with the French against the British. (For an older and different view, which portrays the leading Penobscot sagamore, Joseph Orono, as a "Whig" who had internalized Patriot values, see William D. Williamson, "Notice of Orono" [251].) The military role and contributions of the Wabanakis can best be explored in Frederic Kidder, *Military Operations in Eastern Maine and Nova Scotia During the Revolution* [111], a collection of documents by, and relating to, John Allen, the wartime Superintendent of Eastern Indians for the new republic.

The Indians of southern New England also tended to support the Patriot cause, but for different reasons than those of the north. Through poverty, discrimination, and intermarriage, many of them had become part of the growing underclass of slaves, servants, and free poor, especially non-white, in the older cities and ports. Accordingly, their politics tended to fuse with those of the "lower orders" whose mob activities in the decade before the Revolution frightened even the "respectable" Patriots. Though the role of Indians in these activities remains unstudied, we know a great deal about one of them—Crispus Attucks, the mixed-blood Afro-Indian who, in the Boston massacre of 1770, was the first American to die at the hands of British soldiers. Attucks's Indian ancestry is best documented in J. B. Fisher, "Who Was Crispus Attucks?" [78], but the article is flawed because of Fisher's refusal to recognize that Attucks was a mixed-blood, rather than a "pure" Indian.

The newly Christianized Indians of southwestern New England followed their missionaries and supported the colonists' cause, but the victory soon proved a disillusioning one for them. With small White farmers feeling the economic squeeze that provoked Shays' Rebellion, the pressures on Indians in Stockbridge and elsewhere to give up additional land increased. A strong sense of identity as Indians, albeit as Christian Indians, led many to prefer emigration to continued economic decline and cultural isolation in a predominantly White society. During the mid-1780s, a Christian faction of the Oneida Iroquois invited displaced Indians from elsewhere in the new nation to remove to their lands in New York state. Among those who responded were the Stockbridges, who established New Stockbridge, and members of several Connecticut and Long Island groups, who began Brothertown nearby. The leaders of the two emigrations were, respectively, Hendrick Aupaumut and Samson Occom, by then the two most distinguished Indians in southern New England. Aupaumut's role has been assessed with great sensitivity by Jeanne Ronda and James P. Ronda in "'As They Were Faithful'" [181], and Occom's can be followed in the biographies by Blodgett [15] and Love [124] cited earlier. However, these new communities were short-lived. Increased White settlement in upstate New York forced a new removal in the 1820s, and the Oneida, Stockbridge, and Brothertown Indians all took up new lands in Wisconsin. The story of this last move is told in "Sketch of the Brothertown Indians" [45], by Thomas Commuck, a Narraganset who joined that group shortly before it left New York. An excellent study of the Stockbridge Indians that establishes the underlying continuity in their adaptive strategy from colonial times to the present is Marion Johnson Mochon, "Stockbridge-Munsee Cultural Adaptations" [143].

Tribal Enclaves In a Liberal Republic, 1800–1945

Though the new nation celebrated such abstractions as "liberty" and, before the middle of the nineteenth century, "equality," the Indians of New England quickly found that these terms were not universally applicable. The dominant ethos in American society placed a premium on the autonomy of individual white males, the unhindered workings of a capitalistic market economy, and the striving for material wealth and progress. In this setting, the tiny impoverished communities of Indians struggling to retain their identities and traditions were generally looked upon as anachronisms, when not as actual hindrances to the well-being of others. It is hardly surprising, then, that economic and demographic decline continued apace, Indian lands continued to be alienated, tribal institutions were substantially eroded, and traditional cultures and languages were retained by fewer and fewer individuals. Even so, while some communities disappeared, others maintained a core of tribalism that helped them survive into the twentieth century.

The earliest and strongest expression of tribalism originated in the Cape Cod enclave of Mashpee in the 1830s. The inhabitants of this traditionally independent community sought a return to the relative autonomy they had enjoyed until after the American Revolution. They were led in this effort by the charismatic revivalist preacher, William Apess, a mixed-blood Pequot. Apess presented the Mashpees' legal case, as well as their unique brand of Indian Christianity, with great effectiveness in his *Indian Nullification* [4]. He elaborated his own religious-political views in his autobiography, *A Son of the Forest* [2], in *The Experiences of Five Christian Indians of the Pequod Tribe* [3] and in his militant if somewhat inaccurate view of New England

Indian history, *Eulogy on King Philip* [5], first delivered to an audience of reform-minded Bostonians in 1836. Apess is the subject of a recent essay by Kim McQuaid, "William Apes, Pequot" [139], which finds him relatively successful compared to Indian reformers elsewhere in the United States during the Jacksonian period.*

The White sympathizers who responded to Apess and the Mashpee were not, however, friends of Indian nationalism. They responded primarily to the Indians' Christianity and saw it as a hopeful sign of their eventual assimilation into white society. From this perspective, the Massachusetts government undertook several investigations of its native population during the nineteenth century, the final and most thorough of which was John Milton Earle, *Report to the Governor and Council* [70]. Though laden with the value judgments of an assimilationist, Earle's report is nevertheless a valuable survey of Indian life and communities in the state as of 1861. It should be supplemented by C. G. Woodson, "The Relations of Negroes and Indians in Massachusetts" [255], which not only discusses Afro-Indian miscegenation but also the civil rights and other legislation that followed publication of the Earle report.

Assimilation was also the goal of the Rhode Island

---

*Apess added the second 's' to his surname in the last editions of his work, probably to clarify pronunciation. I have followed his later usage in this essay.

government in its dealings with the Narraganset. Finally, in 1880, it abolished that tribe as a legal entity. As a result, the Narragansets no longer owned land collectively and the legal and educational functions which their council had performed or overseen were now assumed by the state. Nevertheless, as Ethel Boissevain points out in "Detribalization and Group Identity" [17], this move had relatively little effect on the everyday, essentially communal lives of the Indians themselves. The workings of the tribal council shortly before its demise were recorded in "The Minutes and Ledgers of the Narragansett Indians" [19], which have been rediscovered, edited, and thoughtfully analyzed by Boissevain and Ralph Roberts III.

Few sources survive which document the personal lives and thinking of "ordinary" Indians during the period before World War I. One which does is the diary and other fragmentary writings of a Mohegan woman, Fidelia Fielding (1827–1908), from the last decade of her life. These have been edited and commented upon from the perspectives of ethnology and linguistics by Frank G. Speck in "Native Tribes and Dialects of Connecticut" [214]. In her views on religion, nature, and Indian nationalism, as well as in her linguistic expression and the details of her everyday life, Fielding revealed a distinctly and traditionally Indian identity for which assimilation offered no attractions.

Persistent cultural traditions continued to form the basis for a distinctive Indian identity during the first half of this century. In "A Note on the Hassanamisco

Band of Nipmuc" [218], Speck documented a band whose ethnicity remained intact even as its numbers dwindled. And in "Reflections Upon the Past and Present of the Massachusetts Indians" [219], he sought to combat the notion that the cultural survivals of the 1940s were any less legitimate for departing from precontact culture or because Indians had intermarried extensively with Blacks. Similar examples of Indian ethnicity in enclave settings were recorded by Gladys Tantaquidgeon, a Mohegan student of Speck's, in "Notes on the Gay Head Indians" [227], and by Carlos A.H. Westez, a Catawba chief also known as Red Thunder Cloud, in "An Ethnological Introduction to the Long Island Indians" [246]. That oral traditions remained a principal basis for community and continuity is apparent in Mabel Frances Knight's brief collection of "Wampanoag Indian Tales" [112].

In upper New England, the final determination of the international boundary split the Wabanaki Confederacy so that the Penobscots (formerly the Penobscot Abenakis) and Passamaquoddys fell within the United States and the Malecites and Micmacs within Canada. Though the Confederation continued to function until the middle of the nineteenth century, its effectiveness ended earlier as both American tribes split into factions over issues relating to their precarious economies and to religious education. These events are summarized for both tribes in Walker, et al., "A Chronological Account of the Wabanaki Confederacy" [241], and related in greater detail for the Penobscots in Fannie Hardy

Eckstorm, *Old John Neptune and Other Maine Indian Shamans* [74], a highly personal but insightful account of that tribe's history and culture.

Besides Eckstorm's, a second book-length account sought to call attention to those Penobscot traditions that appeared, at the dawn of the twentieth century, to be doomed. Though not published until 1940, Frank G. Speck's *Penobscot Man* [217] was based on field work conducted before World War I. In it, Speck masterfully recorded those aspects of material and social life which represented pre-contact survivals and which differentiated the Penobscot from the dominant culture. Because he deliberately overlooked Euro-American influences, the relative importance of the traditions he describes cannot be assessed from his study alone. Yet the book remains both a classic of early anthropology and a valuable source on native culture at the turn of the century.

Speck reserved for separate publication his studies of Penobscot religion and mythology, "Penobscot Shamanism" [213], an account of beliefs in the power of supernatural magic, and "Penobscot Tales and Religious Beliefs" [216], which included 89 tales as well as an outline of surviving traditions. Several additional collections of tales from northern New England were, like Speck's, occasioned by the recognition that traditional religion and mythology lacked significance for the younger generation. The most complete of these is Charles G. Leland, *The Algonquin Legends of New England* [119], which constitutes a major source for the

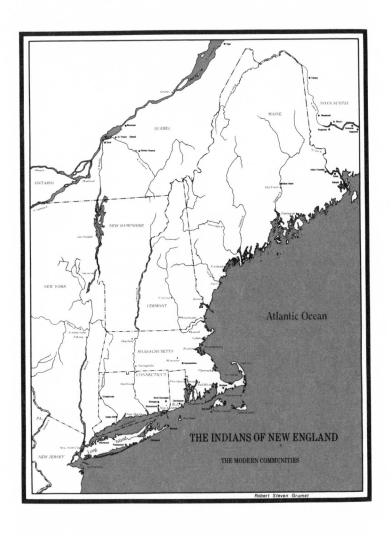

cultural historian, despite Leland's misguided attempts to find Norse and other external connections for the myths. A second good collection is in John Dyneley Prince's bilingual *Passamaquoddy Texts* [169]. A Christian Penobscot's interpretation of these tales is Joseph Nicolar, *The Life and Traditions of the Red Man* [155].

A New Politics

In contrast to the quiet exclusivism of the nineteenth and early twentieth centuries, Indian ethnicity has become increasingly visible to the non-Indian public. As early as 1934, the Narragansets took advantage of the newly passed Indian Reorganization Act and formally "retribalized." In "Narragansett Survival" [16], Ethel Boissevain has described how a cluster of institutions and events highlight an Indian tribal identity that would otherwise be invisible to outsiders. The complexities involved in maintaining such an identity are explored in greater depth in the penetrating essay by Hicks and Kertzer, "Making a Middle Way" [92], which describes a pseudonymous "Monhegan" tribe. The authors emphasize, in particular, the factor of American racial categories in determining the shape of "Monhegan" identity for individual members and for the tribe as a whole.

Indian ethnicity in New England has received additional reinforcement during the last two decades from the nationwide resurgence of tribalism and pan-

Indianism, which has resulted in greater attention to
Indian needs by various governmental agencies, and
from the pressing of land claims cases by several tribes
in the eastern United States. The new political activism
among the Penobscot can be glimpsed in Peter Anastas,
Glooskap's Children [1]. As if uncertain whether to present informative journalism or esoteric literature,
Anastas weaves traditional legends, historical documents, and accounts of his own meetings and experiences with the Penobscot in self-consciously convoluted
fashion. Still, he conveys a strong sense of the ways in
which young Indians of the late 1960s and early 1970s
identified with the history and traditions of their tribe.

A different kind of study linking past and present
is the fine report by Susan MacCulloch Stevens,
"Passamaquoddy Economic Development" [221]. Stevens' assessment of the programs enacted for that tribe
as of 1973, and her proposals for the future, are
rooted in an understanding of Passamaquoddy history
and of the continued primacy among tribal members
of traditional values vis-à-vis those of the dominant culture. A good overview of the social and economic problems of all New England Indians as of the mid-1970s
can be found in Section IIB of Jo Jo Hunt, et al., *Report
on Terminated and Nonfederally Recognized Indians* [95],
prepared for the American Indian Policy Review
Commission. This section surveys each tribe, group,
and organization of Indians, with particular attention
to economic problems, education, and health. Though
census materials are employed, the report relies heavily

on the direct testimony of individual Indians and is, for that reason, an especially valuable document. Additional data on Indians in Connecticut can be found in Keleher and Lamb, *American Indians in Connecticut* [109], which reports on a 1975 state census that corrects the federal count of five years earlier.

The several claims cases are of interest to students of the Indians' past, as well as their present, because they necessarily involve careful reviews of the plaintiff tribes' histories. The Passamaquoddys undertook the first suit, and their arguments and strategy were set out as early as 1971 by O'Toole and Tureen in "State Power and the Passamaquoddy Tribe" [159]. The question of federal recognition as an Indian tribe and its implications for the Passamaquoddys, is fully explored by Tureen in Section V of the *Report on Terminated and Non-federally Recognized Indians* to the Indian Policy Review Commission [95]. A much briefer introduction to all the cases was presented by the Native American Rights Fund in "Eastern Indian Land Claims" [154]. Francis Hutchins, *Mashpee* [96], is a history based largely on materials collected by the defendants in the Mashpee Indians' claims case.

Whereas Indians tended to emigrate from New England during the colonial period, the twentieth century has seen that process reversed. The urban and industrial centers of the region have attracted large numbers of non-New England Indians. Jeanne Guillemin, *Urban Renegades* [89], is a fine sociological study of the largest community of Indian immigrants, the

Micmacs of Boston, that is based primarily on direct field work. Guillemin skillfully demonstrates the persistence of tribalism as an adaptive strategy serving the Micmacs as they move between and among American urban ghettoes and their Canadian reservations.

The history of Indian peoples in the region now called "New England" can be looked at in either (or both) of two ways. On one hand, it is quite obviously a history marked by enormous upheavals and ongoing tragedy — massive mortality, military defeat, geographic dislocation, economic deprivation, and subjection to political systems based on alien cultural values and racist ideologies. (And whether the future holds relief from the poverty and inequality that has prevailed since conquest is by no means certain as of this writing.) Yet the literature surveyed here — chronologically and topically imbalanced as it is — also reveals underlying elements of continuity and triumph. For however transformed, today's Indians are the biological, cultural, and political descendants of peoples who began settling the region 12,000 years ago. Therein lies the quintessential theme of a history that remains less than fully fathomed.

ALPHABETICAL LIST AND INDEX

*Denotes items suitable for secondary school students

[6]   Axtell, James. 1974. "Through a Glass
       Darkly: Colonial Attitudes Toward the
       Native Americans." *American Indian Cul-
       ture and Research Journal* 1(1):17–28.   (20)

[7]   ———. 1978. "The Ethnohistory of
       Early North America: A Review Essay."
       William and Mary Quarterly, 3rd ser.,
       35:110–44.   (13)

[8]   Axtell, James. 1981. *The European and
       the Indian: Essays in the Ethnohistory of
       Colonial North America.* New York: Ox-
       ford University Press.   (19, 27, 40)

[9]   Badger, Stephen. 1798. "Historical and
       Characteristic Traits of the American
       Indians in General, and Those of
       Natick in Particular." *Collections of the
       Massachusetts Historical Society,* 1st ser.,
       5:32–45.   (36)

[10]   Bailey, Alfred Goldsworthy. 1969. *The
       Conflict of European and Eastern Algon-
       kian Cultures, 1504–1700: A Study in
       Canadian Civilization.* 2nd ed. Toronto:
       University of Toronto Press.   (41)

[11]   Banks, Charles Edward. 1911–1925.
       The History of Martha's Vineyard. 3 vols.

Boston: George H. Dean. Reprinted, Edgartown, Mass.: Dukes County Historical Society, 1966. (17)

[12] Bartlett, John Russell, ed. 1856–1865. *Records of the Colony of Rhode Island and Providence Plantations in New England.* 10 vols. Providence: A. Crawford Greene and Brother. Reprinted, New York: AMS, 1968. (17)

[13] Beck, Horace P. 1959. *The American Indian as a Sea-Fighter in Colonial Times.* Mystic, Conn.: Marine Historical Association. (46)

[14] Bennett, M. K. 1955. "The Food Economy of the New England Indians, 1605–75." *Journal of Political Economy* 63:369–97. (8)

[15] Blodgett, Harold. 1935. *Samsom Occom.* Dartmouth College Manuscript Series 3. Hanover, N.H.: Dartmouth College Publications. (40, 50)

[16] Boissevain, Ethel. 1959. "Narragansett Survival: A Study of Group Persistence through Adapted Traits." *Ethnohistory* 6:349–62. (57)

[17]   ———. 1962–63. "Detribalization and Group Identity: the Narragansett Indian Case." *Transactions of the New York Academy of Sciences,* 2nd ser. 25:493–502.   (53)

*[18]   ———. 1975. *The Narragansett People.* Phoenix, Ariz.: Indian Tribal Series, 1975.   (3)

[19]   Boissevain, Ethel, and Ralph Roberts III. 1974. "The Minutes and Ledgers of the Narragansett Indians, 1850–1865: An Intimate Glimpse into the Economic and Social Life of an Acculturated Indian Tribe on the Threshold of Detribalization." *Man in the Northeast* 7:3–28.   (53)

[20]   Bowden, Henry Warner. 1981. *Native Americans and Christian Missions: Studies in Cultural Conflict.* Chicago: University of Chicago Press.   (27)

[21]   Bowden, Henry W., and James P. Ronda, eds. 1980. *John Eliot's Indian Dialogues: A Study in Cultural Interaction.* Westport, Conn.: Greenwood Press.   (29)

[22] Bragdon, Kathleen J. 1979. "Probate Records as a Source for Algonquian Ethnohistory." In *Papers of the Tenth Algonquian Conference,* ed. William Cowan, pp. 136–41. Ottawa: Carleton University. (37)

[23] Brasser, T.J.C. 1966. *Indians of Long Island, 1600–1964.* Colorado Springs: Wanblee Supply Co. (3)

*[24] ———. 1971. "The Coastal Algonkians: People of the First Frontiers." In *North American Indians in Historical Perspective,* eds. Eleanor Burke Leacock and Nancy Oestreich Lurie, pp. 64–91. New York: Random House. (1)

[25] ———. 1978. "Early Indian-European Contacts." In *Northeast,* ed. Bruce G. Trigger, Vol. 15 of *Handbook of North American Indians,* gen. ed. William C. Sturtevant, pp. 78–88. Washington: Government Printing Office. (10)

[26] ———. 1978. "Mahican." In *Northeast,* ed. Bruce G. Trigger, Vol. 15 of *Handbook of North American Indians*, gen. ed. William C. Sturtevant, pp. 198–212. Washington: Government Printing Office. (1)

[27]   Brown, John Marshall. 1890. "The
        Mission of the Assumption on the River
        Kennebec, 1646–1652." *Collections of the
        Maine Historical Society*, 2nd ser. 1:87–
        99.   (45)

[28]   Burton, William John. 1976. "Hellish
        Fiends and Brutish Men: Amer-
        indian-Euroamerican Interaction in
        Southern New England, An Inter-
        disciplinary Analysis, 1600–1750."
        Ph.D. dissertation, Kent State Univer-
        sity. Ann Arbor: University Microfilms.   (18)

[29]   Burton, William, and Richard Lowen-
        thal. 1974. "The First of the Mohe-
        gans." *American Ethnologist* 1:589–99.   (31)

[30]   Butler, Eva L. 1948. "Algonkian Cul-
        ture and Use of Maize in Southern New
        England." *Bulletin of the Archeological
        Society of Connecticut* 22:3–39.   (8)

[31]   Campbell, Paul R., and Glenn W.
        LaFantasie. 1978. "Scattered to the
        Winds of Heaven—Narragansett In-
        dians 1676–1880." *Rhode Island History*
        37:66–83.   (3)

[32] Campeau, Lucien. 1972. *La première mission des Jésuites en Nouvelle-France (1611–1613)*, pp. 11–47. Cahiers d'Histoire des Jésuites 1. Montreal: Les Editions Bellarmin. (12)

[33] Caulkins, Francis Manwaring. 1874. *History of Norwich, Connecticut.* Hartford: Friends of the author. (17)

[34] ———. 1895. *History of New London, Connecticut.* New London: H. D. Utley. (17)

[35] Ceci, Lynn. 1975. "Fish Fertilizer: A Native North American Practice?." *Science* 188 (April 4):26–30. (8)

[36] ———. 1977. "The Effect of European Contact and Trade on the Settlement Pattern of Indians in Coastal New York, 1524–1665: The Archeological and Documentary Evidence." Ph.D. dissertation, City University of New York. Ann Arbor: University Microfilms. (10, 24)

[37] ———. 1978. "Watchers of the Pleiades: Ethnoastronomy and Native Cultivators in Northeastern North America." *Ethnohistory* 25:301–17. (8)

[38]   ———. 1979–80. "The First Fiscal
Crisis in New York." *Economic Development and Cultural Change* 28:839–47.   (24)

[39]   ———. 1979–80. "Maize Cultivation in
Coastal New York: The Archaeological,
Agronomical, and Documentary Evidence." *North American Archaeologist*
1:45–74.   (10)

[40]   Champlain, Samuel de. 1922–1936
[1603–1632]. *The Works of Samuel de
Champlain*, ed. H. P. Biggar. 6 vols. Toronto: The Champlain Society. Reprinted, Toronto and Buffalo: University of Toronto Press, 1971. See vol. 1.   (12)

[41]   Chapin, Howard M. 1931. *Sachems of the
Narragansetts*. Providence: Rhode Island
Historical Society.   (22)

[42]   Charland, Thomas-M. 1964. *Histoire des
Abénakis d'Odanak (1675–1937)*.
Montreal: Editions de Lývrier.   (43)

[43]   Church, Benjamin. 1865. *The History of
King Philip's War,* ed. Henry Martyn
Dexter. Boston: J. K. Wiggin.   (33)

[44]   ———. 1867. *The History of the Eastern Expeditions*, ed. Henry Martyn Dexter. Boston: J. K. Wiggin and Wm. Parsons Lunt.   (36)

[45]   Commuck, Thomas. 1859. "Sketch of the Brothertown Indians." *Collections of the State Historical Society of Wisconsin* 4:291–98.   (50)

[46]   Conkey, Laura E., *et al.* 1978. "Indians of Southern New England and Long Island: Late Period." In *Northeast*, ed. Bruce G. Trigger, Vol. 15 of *Handbook of North American Indians*, gen. ed. William C. Sturtevant, pp. 177–89. Washington: Government Printing Office.   (1)

[47]   Conkling, Robert. 1974. "Legitimacy and Conversion in Social Change: The Case of French Missionaries and the Northeastern Algonkian." *Ethnohistory* 21:1–24.   (43)

[48]   Cook, Sherburne F. 1973. "Interracial Warfare and Population Decline Among the New England Indians." *Ethnohistory* 20:1–24.   (34)

[49]   ———. 1973. "The Significance of Disease in the Extinction of the New England Indians." *Human Biology* 45:485–508.   (13, 19)

[50]   ———. 1976. *The Indian Population of New England in the Seventeenth Century.* University of California Publications in Anthropology 12. Berkeley: University of California Press.   (6)

[51]   Crawford, Michael J. 1978. "Indians, Yankees, and the Meetinghouse Dispute of Natick, Massachusetts, 1743–1800." *New England Historical and Genealogical Register* 132:278–292.   (35)

*[52]   Crosby, Alfred W. 1978. "God . . . Would Destroy Them, and Give Their Country to Another People . . . ," *American Heritage* 29(6):38–43.   (13)

[53]   Daviault, Pierre. 1939. *Le Baron de Saint-Castin, Chef Abénaquis.* Montreal: Editions de l'A.C.-F.   (45)

[54]   Day, Gordon M. 1953. "The Indian as an Ecological Factor in the Northeastern Forest." *Ecology* 34:329–46.   (8)

[55] ———. 1962. "English-Indian Contacts in New England." *Ethnohistory* 9:24–40. (11)

[56] ———. 1965. "The Identity of the Sokokis." *Ethnohistory* 12:237–49. (42)

[57] ———. 1965. "The Indian Occupation of Vermont." *Vermont History* 23:365–74. (42)

[58] ———. 1967. "Historical Notes on New England Languages." In *Contributions to Anthropology: Linguistics I (Algonquian).* National Museum of Canada, Anthropological Series 78, Bulletin 214:107–12. Ottawa. (6)

[59] ———. 1971. "The Eastern Boundary of Iroquoia: Abenaki Evidence." *Man in the Northeast* 1:7–13. (42)

[60] ———. 1973. "Missisquoi: A New Look at an Old Village." *Man in the Northeast* 6:51–57. (42)

[61] ———. 1974. "Henry Tufts as a Source on the Eighteenth Century Abenakis." *Ethnohistory* 21:189–97. (48)

[62] ———. 1978. "Western Abenaki." In *Northeast*, ed. Bruce G. Trigger, Vol. 15 of *Handbook of North American Indians*, gen. ed. William C. Sturtevant, pp. 148–59. Washington: Government Printing Office.   (1)

[63] De Forest, John W. 1853. *History of the Indians of Connecticut: From the Earliest Known Period to 1850.* Hartford: Wm. Jas. Hamersley. Reprinted, Hamden, Conn.: Archon Books, 1964; St. Clair Shores, Mi.: Scholarly, 1970.   (3)

[64] Dincauze, Dena F. 1974. "An Introduction to Archaeology in the Greater Boston Area." *Archaeology of Eastern North America* 2(1):39–67.   (5)

[65] Dorr, Henry C. 1885. "The Narragansetts." *Collections of the Rhode Island Historical Society* 7:135–237.   (21)

[66] Drake, Samuel Adams. 1897. *The Border Wars of New England.* New York: Charles Scribner's Sons. Reprinted, Williamstown, Mass.: Corner House Publishers, 1973.   (46)

[67] Drake, Samuel G. 1857. *Biography and History of the Indians of North America.* 11th ed. Boston: Sanborn, Carter and Bazin. (16)

[68] ———. 1870. *A Particular History of the Five Years French and Indian War in New England and Parts Adjacent.* 11th ed. Boston: S. G. Drake. (46)

[69] Drake, Samuel G. ed. 1839. *Indian Captivities.* Boston: Antiquarian Bookstore and Institute. Reprinted as vol. 55 in The Garland Library of Narratives of North American Indian Captivities, ed. Wilcomb Washburn. New York and London: Garland Publishing Inc., 1976. (46)

[70] Earle, John Milton, 1861. *Report to the Governor and Council, Concerning the Indians of the Commonwealth, Under the Act of April 6, 1859.* Senate Document 96. Boston: William White, Printer to the State. (52)

[71] Eckstorm, Fannie Hardy. 1934. "The Attack on Norridgewock, 1724." *New England Quarterly* 7:541–78. (47)

[72]   ———. 1936. "Pigwacket and Parson
Symmes." *New England Quarterly*
9:378–402.   (47)

[73]   ———. 1939. "Who Was Paugus?" *New
England Quarterly* 12:203–26.   (47)

*[74]   ———. 1945. *Old John Neptune and
Other Maine Indian Shamans.* Portland,
Maine: The Southworth-Anthoensen
Press.   (55)

*[75]   Ellis, George W., and John E. Morris.
1906. *King Philip's War.* New York: The
Grafton Press.   (32)

[76]   Erikson, Vincent O. 1978. "Maliseet-
Passamaquoddy." In *Northeast,* ed.
Bruce G. Trigger, Vol. 15 of *Handbook
of North American Indians* gen. ed.
William C. Sturtevant, pp. 123–36.
Washington: Government Printing
Office.   (1)

[77]   Fenton, William N., *et al.* 1957. *Ameri-
can Indian and White Relations to 1830:
Needs and Opportunities for Study.* Chapel
Hill: University of North Carolina Press
for The Institute of Early American
History and Culture.   (13)

[78] Fisher, J. B. 1872. "Who Was Crispus Attucks?," *American Historical Record* 1 (January):531–33.   (49)

[79] Fitting, James E. 1978. "Regional Cultural Development, 300 B.C. to A.D. 1000." In *Northeast,* ed. Bruce G. Trigger, Vol. 15 of *Handbook of North American Indians,* gen. ed. William C. Sturtevant, pp. 44–57. Washington: Government Printing Office.   (4)

[80] Flannery, Regina. 1939. *An Analysis of Coastal Algonquian Culture.* The Catholic University of America Anthropological Series 7. Washington. Catholic University of America Press.   (7)

[81] Ford, John W., ed. 1896. *Some Correspondence between the Governors and Treasurers of the New England Company. . . .* London: Spottiswood. Reprinted, New York: Burt Franklin, 1970   (38)

[82] Freeman, Frederick. 1858–1862. *The History of Cape Cod: The Annals of Barnstable County, including the District of Mashpee.* 2 vols. Boston: the author.   (17)

[83]   Funk, Robert E. 1978. "Post-Pleistocene
       Adaptations." In *Northeast,* ed. Bruce G.
       Trigger, Vol. 15 of *Handbook of North
       American Indians,* gen ed. William C.
       Sturtevant, pp. 16–27. Washington:
       Government Printing Office.   (4)

[84]   Goddard, Ives. 1978. "Central Algon-
       quian Languages." In *Northeast,* ed.
       Bruce G. Trigger. Vol. 15 of *Handbook
       of North American Indians,* gen. ed.
       William C. Sturtevant, pp. 583–87.
       Washington: Government Printing
       Office.   (6)

[85]   ———. 1978. "Eastern   Algonquian
       Languages." In *Northeast,* ed. Bruce G.
       Trigger, Vol. 15 of *Handbook of North
       American Indians,* gen. ed. William C.
       Sturtevant, pp. 70–77. Washington:
       Government Printing Office.   (6)

*[86] Gookin, Daniel. 1792. "Historical Col-
       lections of the Indians in New En-
       gland." *Collections of the Massachusetts
       Historical Society,* 1st ser. 1:141–227.
       Reprinted, New York: Arno, 1970.   (29)

*[87] ———. 1836. "An Historical Account
       of the Doings and Sufferings of the

Christian Indians in New England, in the Years 1675, 1676, 1677." *Transactions and Collections of the American Antiquarian Society* 2:423–534. Reprinted, New York: Arno, 1972.   (33)

[88] Grumet, Robert Steven. 1980. "Sunksquaws, Shamans, and Tradeswomen: Middle Atlantic Coastal Algonkian Women During the 17th and 18th Centuries." In *Women and Colonization: Anthropological Perspectives,* eds. Mona Etienne and Eleanor Leacock, pp. 43–62. New York: Praeger Scientific.   (9)

[89] Guillemin, Jeanne. 1975. *Urban Renegades: The Cultural Strategy of American Indians.* New York: Columbia University Press.   (59)

*[90] Hare, Lloyd C.M. 1932. *Thomas Mayhew, Patriarch to the Indians (1593–1682).* New York: D. Appleton and Company.   (28)

[91] Herman, Mary W. 1956. "Wampum as a Money in Northeastern North America." *Ethnohistory* 3:21–33.   (24)

[92]   Hicks, George L., and David I. Kertzer. 1972. "Making a Middle Way: Problems of Monhegan Identity." *Southwestern Journal of Anthropology* 28:1–24.   (57)

[93]   Hopkins, Samuel. 1753. *Historical Memoirs, Relating to the Housatunnuk Indians.* Boston: S. Kneeland. Reprinted, New York: Johnson, 1972.   (39)

[94]   Hubbard, William. 1677 *The Present State of New-England, Being a Narrative of the Troubles with the Indians.* London: Printed for Thomas Parkhurst. New ed., edited by Samuel G. Drake as *History of the Indian Wars in New England.* Roxbury, Mass.: W. Eliot Woodward, 1865. Reprinted, New York: Burt Franklin, 1970. Original edition reprinted in facsimile, New York: York Mail Print 1972.   (33)

[95]   Hunt, Jo Jo, *et al.* 1976. *Report on Terminated and Nonfederally Recognized Indians.* Task Force 10. *Final Report to the American Indian Policy Review Commission.* Washington: Government Printing Office.   (58, 59)

*[96] Hutchins, Francis G. 1979. *Mashpee: The Story of Cape Cod's Indian Town*. West Franklin, N.H.: Amarta Press.   (3, 59)

[97] "Indian Treaties," 1853, 1856. *Collections of the Maine Historical Society*, 1st ser. 3:359–447; 4:119–84.   (47)

[98] Jameson, J. Franklin, ed. 1909. *Narratives of New Netherland 1609–1664*. Original Narratives of Early American History. New York: Charles Scribner's Sons. Reprinted, New York: Barnes & Nobel, 1967.   (12)

[99] Jennings, Francis. 1971. "Goals and Functions of Puritan Missions to the Indians," *Ethnohistory* 18:197–212.   (27)

[100] ———. 1971. "Virgin Land and Savage People." *American Quarterly* 23:519–41.   (25)

[101] ———. 1975. *The Invasion of America: Indians, Colonialism, and the Cant of Conquest*. Chapel Hill: University of North Carolina Press. Reprinted, New York: W. W. Norton, 1976.   (20, 32)

[102] Johnson, Margery Ruth. 1966. "The Mayhew Mission to the Indians,

1643–1806." Ph.D. dissertation, Clark University. Ann Arbor: University Microfilms.   (26)

[103] Johnson, Richard R. 1977. "The Search for a Usable Indian: An Aspect of the Defense of Colonial New England." *Journal of American History* 64:623–51.   (36)

[104] Jones, Electa F. 1854. *Stockbridge, Past and Present; or, Records of an Old Mission Station.* Springfield, Mass.: Samuel Bowles and Company.   (38)

*[105] Josselyn, John. 1675. *An Account of Two Voyages to New-England, Made during the years 1638, 1663.* 2nd ed. Boston: William Veazie, 1865.   (23)

[106] Kawashima, Yasuhide. 1969. "Jurisdiction of the Colonial Courts over the Indians in Massachusetts, 1689–1763." *New England Quarterly* 42:532–50.   (35)

[107] ——— 1969. "Legal Origins of the Indian Reservation in Colonial Massachusetts." *American Journal of Legal History* 13:42–56.   (35)

[108] ——— 1977. "Forced Conformity: Puritan Criminal Justice and Indians." *Kansas Law Review* 25:361–73.   (35)

*[109] Keleher, Brendan S., and Trudie Ray Lamb. 1977. *American Indians in Connecticut: A Report of a Statewide Census.* Hartford: Connecticut Indian Affairs Council, Department of Environmental Protection.   (58)

[110] Kellaway, William. 1961. *The New England Company, 1649–1776: Missionary Society to the American Indians.* London: Longmans.   (26)

[111] Kidder, Frederic. 1867. *Military Operations in Eastern Maine and Nova Scotia During the Revolution.* Albany: Joel Munsell. Reprinted, New York: Kraus, 1971.   (48)

*[112] Knight, Mabel Frances. 1925. "Wampanoag Indian Tales." *Journal of American Folk-Lore* 38:134–37.   (54)

[113] Koehler, Lyle. 1979. "Red-White Power Relations and Justice in the Courts of Seventeenth-Century New England."

American Indian Culture and Research Journal 3(4):1–31.   (25)

*[114]   LaFantasie, Glenn W. 1979. "Murder of an Indian, 1638," *Rhode Island History* 38:66–77.   (26)

 [115]   Lauber, Almon Wheeler. 1913. *Indian Slavery in Colonial Times Within the Present Limits of the United States.* Studies in History, Economics and Public Law 134. New York: Columbia University, Faculty of Political Science. Reprinted, Williamstown, Mass.: Corner House Publishers, 1970.   (34)

*[116]   Leach, Douglas Edward. 1958. *Flintlock and Tomahawk: New England in King Philip's War.* New York: Macmillan. Reprinted, New York: W. W. Norton, 1966.   (32)

*[117]   ———. 1966. *The Northern Colonial Frontier, 1607–1763.* New York: Holt, Rinehart and Winston. Reprinted, Albuquerque: University of New Mexico Press, 1974.   (15)

 [118]   Leger, Sister Mary Celeste. 1929. *The Catholic Indian Missions in Maine*

(1611–1820). Catholic University of America Studies in American Church History 8. Washington: Catholic University of America Press.   (43)

[119] Leland, Charles G. 1884. *The Algonquin Legends of New England or Myths and Folklore of the Micmac, Passamaquoddy, and Penobscot Tribes.* Boston: Houghton, Mifflin and Company.   (55)

[120] Lescarbot, Marc. 1907–1914 [1609]. *The History of New France,* trans. and ed. W. L. Grant and intro. by H.P. Biggar. 3 vols. Toronto: The Champlain Society. Reprinted, New York: Greenwood Press, 1968.   (12)

[121] Levermore, Charles Herbert, ed. 1912. *Forerunners and Competitors of the Pilgrims and Puritans.* 2 vols. Brooklyn: New England Society of Brooklyn.   (12)

[122] Lewis, Alonzo, and James R. Newhall. 1865. *History of Lynn, Essex County, Massachusetts.* Boston: John L. Shorey.   (17)

[123] Lincoln, Charles H., ed. 1913. *Narratives of the Indian Wars, 1675–1699.* New York: Charles Scribner's Sons. Re-

printed, New York: Barnes and Noble, 1966.   (33)

[124]   Love, W. DeLoss. 1899. *Samson Occom and the Christian Indians of New England.* Boston and Chicago: The Pilgrim Press.   (50)

[125]   MacCulloch, Susan L. 1966. "A Tripartite Political System among Christian Indians of Early Massachusetts." *Kroeber Anthropological Society Papers* 34 (Spring):63–73.   (28)

[126]   Maine Historical Society. 1869–1916. *Documentary History of the State of Maine.* Collections of the Maine Historical Society, 2nd ser. 24 vols. Portland: Maine Historical Society.   (47)

[127]   Malone, Patrick M. 1973. "Changing Military Technology Among the Indians of Southern New England, 1600– 1677." *American Quarterly* 25:48–63.   (33)

[128]   Marten, Catherine. 1970. *The Wampanoags in the Seventeenth Century: An Ethnohistorical Survey.* Occasional Papers in Old Colony Studies 2. Plymouth, Mass.: Plimoth Plantation.   (7)

[129] Martin, Calvin. 1973. "Fire and Forest Structure in the Aboriginal Eastern Forest." *Indian Historian* 6(4):38–42, 54. (8)

[130] Mason, Van Wyck. 1938. "Bermuda's Pequots." *Bulletin of the Archeological Society of Connecticut* 7:12–16. (34)

[131] Massachusetts Historical Society. 1834. "Tracts Relating to the Attempts to Convert to Christianity the Indians of New England." In *Collections of the Massachusetts Historical Society,* 3rd ser. 4:1–287. (29)

[132] Mather, Increase. 1676. *A Brief History of the War with the Indians in New-England.* London: Printed for Richard Chiswell. Edited by Samuel G. Drake as *The History of King Philip's War.* Albany: J. Munsell, 1862. (33)

[133] ———. 1677. *A Relation of the Troubles which Have happened in New-England.* Boston: John Foster. Edited by Samuel G. Drake as *Early History of New England.* Boston: For the editor, 1864. (33)

[134] Maurault, Joseph. 1866. *Histoire des Abénakis, depuis 1605 jusqu'a nos jours.*

Sorel, Que.: L'Atelier Typographique de la "Gazette de Sorel."   (42)

[135] Mayhew, Experience. 1727. *Indian Converts.* London: printed for S. Gerrish. (29, 37)

[136] McCallum, James Dow. 1939. *Eleazar Wheelock: Founder of Dartmouth College.* Dartmouth College Manuscript Series 4. Hanover, N.H.: Dartmouth College Publications.   (40)

[137] McCallum, James Dow, ed. 1932. *The Letters of Eleazar Wheelock's Indians.* Dartmouth College Manuscript Series 1. Hanover, N.H.: Dartmouth College Publications.   (40)

[138] McManis, Douglas R. 1972. *European Impressions of the New England Coast, 1497–1620.* Research Paper 139. Chicago: University of Chicago, Department of Geography.   (11)

*[139] McQuaid, Kim. 1977. "William Apes, Pequot: An Indian Reformer in the Jackson Era." *New England Quarterly* 50:605–625.   (52)

[140] Means, Carroll Alton. 1947. "Mohegan-Pequot Relationships, as Indicated by the Events Leading to the Pequot Massacre of 1637 and Subsequent Claims in the Mohegan Land Controversy." *Bulletin of the Archeological Society of Connecticut* 21:26–34.   (30)

[141] Meserve, Walter T. 1956. "English Works of Seventeenth-Century Indians." *American Quarterly* 8:264–76.   (28)

[142] Metcalf, P. Richard. 1974. "Who Should Rule at Home? Native American Politics and Indian-White Relations." *Journal of American History* 61:651–65.   (31)

[143] Mochon, Marion Johnson. 1968. "Stockbridge-Munsee Cultural Adaptations: 'Assimilated Indians'." *Proceedings of the American Philosophical Society* 112:182–219.   (50)

[144] Moloney, Francis X. 1931. *The Fur Trade in New England, 1620–1676.* Harvard Undergraduate Essays. Cambridge, Mass.: Harvard University Press.   (23)

[145]   Morrison, Alvin H. 1975. "Membertou's Raid on the Chouacoet
'Almouchiquois'—The Micmac Sack of
Saco in 1607." In *Papers of the Sixth Algonquian Conference, 1974,* ed. William
Cowan, National Museum of Man Mer-
cury Series, Canadian Ethnology Paper
23, pp. 141–58. Ottawa: National
Museums of Canada.   (12)

[146]   Morrison, Kenneth M. 1974. "'That
Art of Coyning Christians': John Eliot
and the Praying Indians of Massachusetts." *Ethnohistory* 21:77–92.   (27)

[147]   ———. 1974. "Sebastien Racle and
Norridgewock, 1724: The Eckstorm
Conspiracy Thesis Reconsidered."
Maine Historical Society Quarterly
14:76–97.   (47)

[148]   ———. 1975. "The People of the
Dawn: The Abnaki and their Relations
with New England and New France,
1600–1727." Ph.D. dissertation, University of Maine. Ann Arbor: University Microfilms.   (41)

[149]   ———. 1979. "Towards a History of
Intimate Encounters: Algonkian

Folklore, Jesuit Missionaries, and
Kiwakwe, The Cannibal Giant." *American Indian Culture and Research Journal*
3(4):51–80. (43)

[150] ——. 1980. "The Bias of Colonial
Law: English Paranoia and the Abenaki
Arena of King Philip's War, 1675–
1678." *The New England Quarterly*
53:363–87. (45)

[151] Morton, Thomas. 1637. *New English
Canaan or New Canaan*. Amsterdam:
Jacob Frederick Stam. New ed., ed.
Charles Francis Adams, Jr., Boston:
The Prince Society, 1883. Reprinted,
New York: Burt Franklin, 1967. (23)

[152] Munson, Graham. 1965. "St. Castin: A
Legend Revised." *Dalhousie Review*
16:338–60. (45)

*[153] Nash, Gary B. 1974. *Red, White, and
Black: The Peoples of Early America*.
Englewood Cliffs, N.J.: Prentice Hall.
2nd ed., 1982. (14)

[154] Native American Rights Fund. 1977.
"Eastern Indian Land Claims." *Announcements* (August):1–21. (59)

[155]   Nicolar, Joseph. 1893. *The Life and
        Traditions of the Red Man.* Bangor, Me.:
        C. H. Glass & Co. Reprinted, Frederic-
        ton, N.B.: Saint Annes Point Press,
        1979.   (57)

[156]   Occom, Samson. 1809 [1761]. "Account
        of the Montauk Indians on Long Is-
        land." In *Collections of the Massachusetts
        Historical Society*, 1st ser. 10:106–11.   (37)

[157]   Orcutt, Samuel. 1882. *The Indians of the
        Housatonic and Naugatuck Valleys.*
        Hartford: Case, Lockwood & Brainard.   (39)

[158]   Orr, Charles, ed. 1897. *History of the
        Pequot War.* Cleveland: The Helman-
        Taylor Co.   (31)

[159]   O'Toole, Francis J., and Thomas N.
        Tureen. 1971. "State Power and the
        Passamaquoddy Tribe: 'A Gross Na-
        tional Hypocrisy?'." *Maine Law Review*
        23:1–39.   (59)

[160]   Palfrey, John Gorham. 1858–1890. *His-
        tory of New England.* 5 vols. Boston: Lit-
        tle, Brown, and Company.   (16)

[161]   Parkman, Francis. 1865. *Pioneers of
        France in the New World, France and Eng-*

land in North America, 1. Boston: Little, Brown, and Company. Many editions available. (16)

[162] ———. 1867. *The Jesuits in North America in the Seventeenth Century, France and England in North America* 2. Boston: Little, Brown, and Company. Reprinted, New York: F. Ungar, 1965. Many editions available. (16)

[163] ———. 1877. *Count Frontenac and New France under Louis XIV, France and England in North America* 5. Boston: Little, Brown and Company. Reprinted, New York: F. Ungar, 1965. Many editions available. (16)

[164] ———. 1884. *Montcalm and Wolfe*, 2 vols., *France and England in North America* 7. Boston, Little, Brown, and Company. Many editions available. (16)

[165] ———. 1892. *A Half-Century of Conflict*, 2 vols., *France and England in North America* 6. Boston: Little, Brown, and Company. Many editions available. (16)

[166] Penhallow, Samuel. 1726. *The History of the Wars of New-England, With the Eastern*

Indians. Boston: Printed by T. Fleet for S. Gerrish and D. Henchman. New edition printed as *Penhallow's Indian Wars*, ed. Edward Wheelock. Boston: E. Wheelock, 1924. Reprinted, Williamstown, Mass.: Corner House Publishers, 1973.   (46)

[167] Pilling, James Constantine. 1891. *Bibliography of the Algonquian Languages.* Bureau of American Ethnology Bulletin 13. Washington: Government Printing Office.   (6)

[168] Potter, Elisha R., Jr., 1835. *The Early History of Narragansett.* In *Collections of the Rhode Island Historical Society* 3.   (21)

[169] Prince, John Dyneley. 1921. *Passamaquoddy Texts.* Publications of the American Ethnological Society, ed. Franz Boas, vol. 10. New York: G. E. Stechert & Co.   (44, 57)

*[170] Quinn, David B. 1977. *North America from Earliest Discovery to First Settlements: The Norse Voyages to 1612.* New York: Harper & Row.   (11)

[171] Rainey, Froelich G. 1936. "A Compilation of Historical Data Contributing to

the Ethnography of Connecticut and Southern New England Indians." *Bulletin of the Archeological Society of Connecticut* 3:1–89. Reprinted, 1956.　　(7)

[172] Rawson, Grindal, and Samuel Danforth. 1809. "Account of an Indian Visitation, A.D. 1698," ed. Gideon Hawley. In *Collections of the Massachusetts Historical Society,* 1st ser. 10:129–34.　　(37)

[173] Richardson, Leon Burr, ed. 1933. *An Indian Preacher in England.* Dartmouth College Manuscript Series 2. Hanover, N.H.: Dartmouth College Publications.　　(40)

[174] Ritchie, William A. 1969. *The Archaeology of Martha's Vineyard, A Framework for the Prehistory of Southern New England: A Study in Coastal Ecology and Adaptation.* Garden City, N.Y.: Natural History Press.　　(5)

[175] Robbins, Maurice. 1956. "Indians of the Old Colony; Their Relation with and Their Contributions to the Settlement of the Area." *Bulletin of the Massachusetts Archaeological Society* 17:59–74.　　(22)

[176] Roberts, William I., III. 1958. "The Fur Trade of New England in the Seven-

teenth Century." Ph.D. dissertation, University of Pennsylvania. Ann Arbor: University Microfilms.   (23)

[177] Ronda, James P. 1977. "Red and White at the Bench: Indians and the Law in Plymouth Colony." *Essex Institute Historical Collections* 25:361–73.   (25)

[178] ———. 1977. "'We Are Well as We Are': An Indian Critique of Seventeenth-Century Christian Missions." *William and Mary Quarterly,* 3rd ser. 34:66–82.   (28)

[179] ———. 1981. "Generations of Faith: The Christian Indians of Martha's Vineyard." *William and Mary Quarterly,* 3rd ser. 38: in press.   (30)

[180] Ronda, James P., and Jeanne Ronda. 1975. "The Death of John Sassamon: An Exploration in Writing New England History." *American Indian Quarterly* 1:91–102.   (32)

[181] Ronda, Jeanne, and James P. Ronda. 1979. "'As They Were Faithful': Chief Hendrick Aupaumut and the Struggle for Stockbridge Survival, 1757–1830."

American Indian Culture and Research Journal 3(3):43–55. (50)

[182] Russell, Howard S. 1980. *Indian New England Before the Mayflower.* Hanover, N.H. and London: University Press of New England. (7)

[183] Sainsbury, John A. 1971. "Miantonomo's Death and New England Politics 1630–1645." *Rhode Island History* 30:111–23. (32)

[184] ———. 1975. "Indian Labor in Early Rhode Island." *New England Quarterly* 48:378–93. (36)

[185] Salisbury, Neal. 1972. "Conquest of the 'Savage': Puritans, Puritan Missionaries, and Indians, 1620–1680." Ph.D. dissertation, University of California, Los Angeles. Ann Arbor: University Microfilms. (20)

[186] ———. 1974. "Red Puritans: The 'Praying Indians' of Massachusetts Bay and John Eliot." *William and Mary Quarterly,* 3rd ser. 31:27–54. (27)

*[187] ———. 1981. "Squanto: Last of the Patuxets." In *Struggle and Survival in*

Colonial America. eds. David G. Sweet and Gary B. Nash. Berkeley: University of California Press.   (10)

[188]   ———. 1981. *Manitou and Providence: Indians, Europeans, and the Making of New England, 1500–1643.* New York: Oxford University Press.   (10, 21)

[189]   Salwen, Bert. 1969. "A Tentative 'In Situ' Solution to the Mohegan-Pequot Problem." In *An Introduction to the Archaeology and History of the Connecticut Valley Indian*, ed. William K. Young, pp. 81–88. Springfield, Mass.: Springfield Museum of Science.   (30)

[190]   ———. 1978. "Indians of Southern New England and Long Island: Early Period." In *Northeast*, ed. Bruce G. Trigger, Vol. 15 of *Handbook of North American Indians*, gen. ed. William C. Sturtevant, pp. 160–76. Washington: Government Printing Office.   (1, 21)

[191]   Sehr, Timothy J. 1977. "Ninigret's Tactics of Accommodation—Indian Diplomacy in New England, 1637–1675." *Rhode Island History* 36:42–53.   (32)

[192]   Sévigny, P.-André. 1976. *Les Abénaquis:*
        Habitat et migrations (17ᵉ et 18ᵉ siècles),
        Cahiers d'Histoire des Jesuites 3.
        Montreal: Les Éditions Bellarmin.   (42)

[193]   Sheldon, George. 1895–1896. *A History*
        of Deerfield, Massachusetts. 2 vols. Deer-
        field, Mass. [Greenfield, Mass.]: Press of
        E. A. Hall & Co. Reprinted in facsimile,
        Somersworth: New Hampshire Publish-
        ing Company, 1972.   (17)

[194]   Shuffelton, Frank. 1976. "Indian Devils
        and Pilgrim Fathers: Squanto,
        Hobomok, and the English Conception
        of Indian Religion." *New England Quar-*
        terly 49:108–16.   (27)

[195]   Shurtleff, Nathaniel B., ed. 1853–1854.
        Records of the Governor and Company of
        the Massachusetts Bay in New England. 5
        vols. Boston: William White. Reprinted,
        New York: AMS, 1968.   (17)

[196]   Shurtleff, Nathaniel B., and David Pul-
        sifer, eds. 1855–1861. *Records of the*
        Colony of New Plymouth in New England.
        12 vols. Boston: William White. Re-
        printed, New York: AMS, 1968.   (17)

[197]   Simmons, William Scranton. 1970. *Cautantowwit's House: An Indian Burial Ground on the Island of Conanicut in Narragansett Bay*. Providence: Brown University Press, 1970.   (9)

[198]   ———. 1976. "Southern New England Shamanism: An Ethnographic Reconstruction." In *Papers of the Seventh Algonquian Conference, 1975*, ed. William Cowan, pp. 217–56. Ottawa: Carleton University.   (9)

[199]   ———. 1978. "Narragansett." In *Northeast*, ed. Bruce G. Trigger, Vol 15 of *Handbook of North American Indians*, gen. ed. William C. Sturtevant, pp. 190–97. Washington: Government Printing Office.   (1)

[200]   ———. 1979. "Conversion from Indian to Puritan." *New England Quarterly* 52:197–218.   (28)

[201]   ———. 1979. "The Great Awakening and Indian Conversion in Southern New England." In *Papers of the Tenth Algonquian Conference*, ed. William Cowan, pp. 25–36. Ottawa: Carleton University.   (39)

[202] ———. 1981. "Cultural Bias in the New England Puritans' Perception of Indians." *William and Mary Quarterly*, 3rd ser. 38:56–72. (x)

[203] Slotkin, J. S., and Karl Schmitt. 1949. "Studies of Wampum." *American Anthropologist*, new ser. 51:223–36. (24)

[204] Smith, John. 1910. *Travels and Works of Captain John Smith*, ed. Edward Arber. 2 vols. Edinburgh: John Grant. (12)

[205] Smith, Joseph Henry. 1950. *Appeals to the Privy Council from the American Plantations*. New York: Columbia University Press. Reprinted, New York: Octagon Books, 1965. (36)

[206] Snow, Dean R. 1968. "Wabanaki 'Family Hunting Territories'." *American Anthropologist*, new ser. 70:1143–51. (9)

[207] ———. 1976. "Abenaki Fur Trade in the Sixteenth Century." *Western Canadian Journal of Anthropology* 6:3–11. (12)

[208] ———. 1978. "Eastern Abenaki." In *Northeast*, ed. Bruce G. Trigger, Vol. 15 of *Handbook of North American Indians*,

gen ed. William C. Sturtevant, pp. 137–47. Washington: Government Printing Office. (1)

[209] ——. 1978. "Late Prehistory of the East Coast." In *Northeast*, ed. Bruce G. Trigger, Vol. 15 of *Handbook of North American Indians*, gen. ed. William C. Sturtevant, pp. 58–69. Washington: Government Printing Office. (4)

[210] ——. 1980. *The Archaeology of New England*. New York: Academic Press. (5)

[211] Speck, Frank G. 1915. "The Eastern Algonkian Wabanaki Confederacy." *American Anthropologist*, new ser. 17:492–508. (44)

[212] ——. 1919. "The Functions of Wampum among the Eastern Algonkian." *Memoirs of the American Anthropological Association* 6:3–71. (44)

[213] ——. 1919. "Penobscot Shamanism." *Memoirs of the American Anthropological Association* 6:238–88. (55)

[214] ——. 1928. "Native Tribes and Dialects of Connecticut: A Mohegan-

Pequot Diary." In *Forty-Third Annual Report of the Bureau of American Ethnology, 1925–1926*, pp. 199–287. Washington: Government Printing Office. (53)

[215] ———. 1928. *Territorial Subdivisions and Boundaries of the Wampanoag, Massachusett, and Nauset Indians*. Indian Notes and Monographs 44. New York: Museum of the American Indian, Heye Foundation. (7)

[216] ———. 1935. "Penobscot Tales and Religious Beliefs." *Journal of American Folk-Lore* 48:1–107. (55)

[217] ———. 1940. *Penobscot Man: The Life History of a Forest Tribe in Maine*. Philadelphia: University of Pennsylvania Press. Reprinted, New York: Octagon Books, 1970. (55)

[218] ———. 1943. "A Note on the Hassanamisco Band of Nipmuc." *Bulletin of the Massachusetts Archaeological Society* 4(4):49–56. (54)

[219] ———. 1943. "Reflections Upon the Past and Present of the Massachusetts Indians." *Bulletin of the Massachusetts Archaeological Society* 4(3):33–38. (54)

[220]   Starbuck, Alexander. 1924. *The History of Nantucket, County, Island and Town.* Boston: C. E. Goodspeed & Co. Reprinted, Rutland, Vt.: C. E. Tuttle, Co., 1969.   (17)

[221]   Stevens, Susan MacCulloch. 1978. "Passamaquoddy Economic Development in Cultural and Historic Perspective." In *American Indian Economic Development,* ed. Sam Stanley, pp. 313–408. The Hague and Paris: Mouton.   (58)

[222]   Stineback, David C. 1978. "The Status of Puritan-Indian Scholarship." *New England Quarterly* 51:80–90.   (21)

[223]   Stone, William L. 1842. *Uncas and Miantonomoh.* New York: Dayton & Newman.   (32)

[224]   Sturtevant, William C. 1975. "Two 1761 Wigwams at Niantic, Connecticut." *American Antiquity* 40:437–44.   (37)

[225]   Sylvester, Herbert Milton. 1910. *Indian Wars of New England.* 3 vols. Boston: W. B. Clarke; Cleveland: Arthur H. Clarke. Reprinted, New York: Arno, 1979.   (15, 46)

[226] Szasz, Margaret Connell. 1980. "'Poor Richard' Meets the Native American: Schooling for Young Indian Women in Eighteenth-Century Connecticut." *Pacific Historical Review* 49:215–35. (40)

[227] Tantaquidgeon, Gladys. 1930. "Notes on the Gay Head Indians of Massachusetts." Museum of the American Indian, Heye Foundation. *Indian Notes* 7(1);1–26. (54)

[228] Temple, Josiah H. 1887. *History of North Brookfield, Massachusetts.* North Brookfield: the author. (17)

[229] Temple, J. H. and George Sheldon. 1875. *History of the Town of Northfield, Massachusetts.* Albany, N.Y.: Joel Munsell. (17)

[230] Thomas, Peter Allen. 1973. "Squakheag Ethnohistory: A Preliminary Study of Culture Conflict on the Seventeenth Century Frontier." *Man in the Northeast* 5:27–36. (43)

[231] ———. 1976. "Contrastive Subsistence Strategies and Land Use as Factors for Understanding Indian-White Relations in New England." *Ethnohistory* 23:1–18. (8)

[232]   ———. 1979. "In the Maelstrom of
Change: The Indian Trade and Cultural Process in the Middle Connecticut
River Valley, 1635–1665." Ph.D. dissertation, University of Massachusetts.   (23)

[233]   Thwaites, Reuben Gold, ed. 1896–
1901. *The Jesuit Relations and Allied Documents: Travels and Explorations of the
Jesuit Missionaries in New France, 1610–
1791.* 73 vols. Cleveland: The Burrows
Brothers Company. Reprinted in 36
vols., New York: Pageant Book Company, 1959. See vols. 1–4, 36, 38, 67 of
original edition.   (12, 44, 47)

[234]   Townshend, Charles Hervey. 1900.
"The Quinnipiack Indians and their
Reservation." *New Haven Colony Histori-
cal Society Papers* 6:151–219.   (27)

[235]   Trelease, Allen W. 1960. *Indian Affairs
in Colonial New York: The Seventeenth
Century.* Ithaca, N.Y.: Cornell University Press. Reprinted, Port Washington,
N.Y.: Kennikat Press, 1970.   (22)

[236]   Trigger, Bruce G., ed. 1978. *Northeast,*
Vol. 15 of *Handbook of North American
Indians,* gen. ed. William C. Sturtevant.

20 vols. Washington: Government
Printing Office. See [25] [26] [46] [62]
[76] [79] [83] [84] [85] [190] [199] [208]
[209] [238] [243].   (1)

[237] Trumbull, J. Hammond, ed. 1850–
1890. *The Public Records of the Colony of
Connecticut.* 15 vols. Hartford: Brown
and Parson. Reprinted, New York:
AMS and Johnson Reprint Corp., 1968. (17)

[238] Tuck, James A. 1978. "Regional Cultural Development, 3000 to 300 B.C."
In *Northeast,* ed. Bruce G. Trigger, Vol.
15 of *Handbook of North American Indians,* gen ed. William C. Sturtevant, pp.
28–43. Washington: Government Print-
ing Office.   (4)

[239] Vaughan, Alden T. 1965. *New England
Frontier: Puritans and Indians, 1620–
1675.* Revised ed., New York and Lon-
don: W. W. Norton, 1979.   (20)

[240] Vaughan, Alden T., and Daniel K.
Richter. 1980. "Crossing the Cultural
Divide: Indians and New Englanders,
1605–1763." *Proceedings of the American
Antiquarian Society* 90:23–.   (15)

[241]   Walker, Willard, et al. 1980. "A Chronological Account of the Wabanaki Confederacy." In *Political Organization of Native Americans,* ed. Ernest L. Schusky, pp. 41–84. Washington: University Press of America.   (44, 48, 54)

[242]   Warner, Frederic W. 1972. "The Foods of the Connecticut Indians." *Bulletin of the Archaeological Society of Connecticut* 37:27–47.   (8)

[243]   Washburn, Wilcomb E. 1978. "Seventeenth-Century Indian Wars." In *Northeast,* ed. Bruce G. Trigger, Vol. 15 of *Handbook of North American Indians,* gen. ed. William C. Sturtevant, pp. 89–100. Washington: Government Printing Office.   (30)

[244]   Weeden, William B. 1884. *Indian Money as a Factor in New England Civilization.* Johns Hopkins University Studies in Historical and Political Science, 2nd ser. 8–9.   (24)

[245]   Weis, Frederick L. 1947–51. "The New England Company of 1649 and its Missionary Enterprises." *Publications of the Colonial Society of Massachusetts, Transactions* 38:134–218.   (26)

[246] Westez, Carlos A.H. [Red Thunder Cloud]. 1945. "An Ethnological Introduction to the Long Island Indians." *Bulletin of the Massachusetts Archaeological Society* 6(3):39–42. (54)

[247] Whiting, B.J. 1947. "Incident at Quantabacook, March, 1764." *New England Quarterly* 20:169–96. (48)

[248] Williams, John. 1707. *The Redeemed Captive Returning to Zion.* Boston: Printed by Bartholomew Green for Samuel Phillips. New ed, edited by Edward W. Clark as *The Redeemed Captive.* Amherst: University of Massachusetts Press, 1976. Many reprints of original available. (46)

[249] Williams, Lorraine E. 1972. "Ft. Shantok and Ft. Corchaug: A Comparative Study of Seventeenth Century Culture Contact in the Long Island Sound Area." Ph.D. dissertation, New York University. Ann Arbor: University Microfilms. (19)

[250] Williams, Roger. 1643. *A Key into the Language of America.* London: Gregory Dexter. New ed., ed. John J. Teunissen

and Evelyn J. Hinz. Detroit: Wayne
State University Press, 1973.   (22)

[251]   Williamson, William D. 1846. "Notice
of Orono, a Chief at Penobscot." *Collections of the Massachusetts Historical Society,*
3rd ser. 9:82–91.   (48)

[252]   Willoughby, Charles C. 1935. *Antiquities
of the New England Indians, With Notes on
the Ancient Cultures of the Adjacent Territories.* Cambridge, Mass.: Harvard
University, Peabody Museum of American Archaeology and Ethnology. Reprinted, New York: AMS, 1973.   (6)

[253]   Winslow, Edward. 1624. *Good News from
New England.* London: W. Bladen and
J. Bellamie. New ed. in *Chronicles of the
Pilgrim Fathers,* ed. Alexander Young,
pp. 269–375. Boston: Charles C. Little
and James Brown, 1841. Reprinted,
New York: Da Capo, 1971.   (22)

[254]   Wood, William. 1634. *New England's
Prospect.* London: Tho. Cotes, for John
Bellamie. New ed, ed. Alden T.
Vaughan, Amherst: University of
Massachusetts Press, 1977.   (22)

[255] Woodson, C. G. 1920. "The Relations of Negroes and Indians in Massachusetts." *Journal of Negro History* 5:45–62.   (52)

[256] Wright, Harry Andrew. 1941. "The Technique of Seventeenth Century Indian-Land Purchasers." *Essex Institute Historical Collections* 77:185–97.   (25)

[257] Wroth, Lawrence C., ed. and trans. 1970. *The Voyages of Giovanni de Verrazzano, 1524–1528.* New Haven and London: Yale University Press.   (11)